SEO Keyword Strategy

How to Select Keywords for Your Search Engine Optimization Campaign

First Edition

Gajan Retnasaba
Thomas Parker
Meyling Lau

SEO Keyword Strategy

How to Select Keywords for Your Search Engine Optimization Campaign.

First Edition

This book is intended to help readers identify the optimal set of keywords for a search engine optimization campaign. The information in this book is based on the experience and opinions of the authors.

Inquiries should be addressed to: book@seomap.com.

ISBN 978-0-9858720-0-7

The authors greatly appreciate the assistance of our compositor Barbara Alber, our cover artist Wes Riojas, and our editor Lois Gourley. We are blessed to have you on our team.

Table of Contents

Table of Contents (continued)

1 Introduction

"A journey of a thousand miles begins by pointing yourself in the right direction."
Adapted from Laozi, *Philosopher* (604 BC - 531 BC).

SEO is a war fought to secure valuable territory at the top of the Google Search listings. The war consists of a number of battles to wrest individual keywords like *lawnmower*, or *riding mower* from the grasp of competitors. In the frenzy of war, a successful general thinks strategically. Not all battles are equal. Some battles yield the high ground or access to an important bridge. Other battles yield naught but the right to call yourself the victor. Some battles are won simply by firing a couple of warning shots. Other battles result in long arduous sieges — battling against a well-fortified garrison determined to fight down to the last man. And sometimes the best outcomes are achieved not by battle at all, but by diplomacy, espionage, or even surrender.

For the small business owner, a well-thought-out strategy will help your nimble business outflank a sclerotic mega-corporation in the war for traffic. Just like Alexander at Issus, you can make up for your lack of numbers with precise targeted attacks.

For the Fortune 500 company, a sound strategy will help management efficiently deploy resources to steamroll the gaggle of upstarts. Like the allies in Desert Storm, use your massive resource advantage to quickly overwhelm the opposition and take territory with minimal casualties.

The keyword strategy provides the battle orders for an SEO campaign. The keyword strategy gives you a plan to direct your troops so that they fight in battles where the odds are in your favor and where victory will prove most advantageous. Just as importantly, a sound keyword strategy avoids Pyrrhic Wars, where the battles are fierce and the rewards are meager. While a keyword strategy alone will not carry you to a bountiful victory, it can tilt the odds in your favor.

The objective of an SEO keyword strategy is to select the keywords and keyword phrases to target with your SEO campaign. Simply put, you are choosing the keywords and keyword phrases for which you want to rank highly in Google, Bing, and other search engines. SEO investment returns are maximized by strategically selecting the keywords that represent the best opportunities.

Most companies have thousands of potentially relevant search terms where ranking well would improve their business, but only some of these search terms represent economically viable opportunities. Should your doll shop optimize for the keyword *doll*, *baby doll*, *porcelain baby doll*, or some other keyword you haven't even thought about? The problem you face is twofold. Firstly, it is an identification problem: How do you find all the potentially useful keywords that could be relevant to your business? And secondly, it is an evaluation problem: How do you sift through all these keywords and select the set of keywords that will provide the greatest return on investment?

This book describes a process for developing your keyword strategy. You will learn how to generate a comprehensive set of relevant candidate keywords, and how to analyze and evaluate those candidate keywords. This allows you to determine the optimal set of keywords for your SEO campaign. This keyword strategy will inform your SEO campaign, determining the pages you create, the keywords you embed in your content, and the links you build. This book helps you define your keyword strategy so that when you begin the hard work of an SEO campaign you fight smart as well as hard.

Before going any further, let us back up and provide some background on the nature of SEO and the role played by a sound keyword strategy.

What is SEO?

Search Engine Optimization (SEO) is a marketing technique designed to attract traffic to a website by making the webpages appear more prominently (for specific keywords and keyword phrases) in the unpaid search results of search engines like Google, Bing, and Yahoo.

Search engines return a list of websites that are relevant to a user query. Along the top and side of the search results page, search engines list websites that pay to be included in the search results. Companies with *paid listings*, also known as Pay-Per-Click (PPC) listings, are charged by the search engines each time someone clicks on their advertisement. But, on the prime real estate in the middle of the page, search engines display the websites they deem to be the most trusted and most relevant to the user for that query. Unlike paid listings, these results are provided at no cost to the listed websites. These free listings, known as *organic listings*, are the recipients of the majority of search engine traffic. Consequently, being perceived as the most trusted and most relevant website for a particular search can be a lucrative source of traffic.

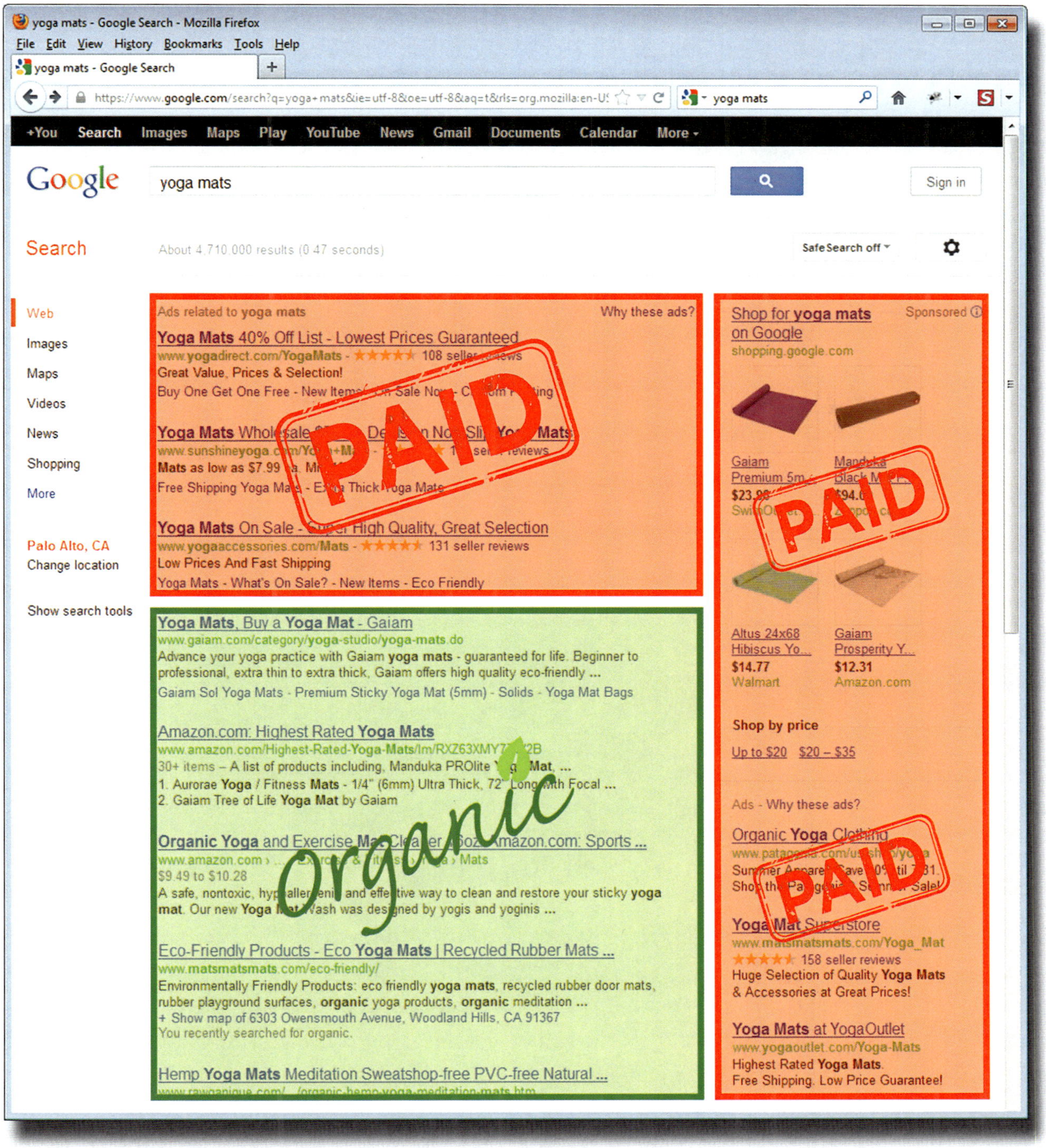

Figure 1 – Google search results with Paid Listings and Organic Listings.

SEO is a set of techniques designed to elevate a website's position in the organic listings. SEO is an attempt to persuade the search engines that your website is the most trusted and most relevant source of information on various keywords, and thereby will enhance the user experience if it is displayed at the top of the organic listings.

Having a website listed in these free organic listings is valuable because two times more clicks go to the organic listings (56%) than go to the paid listings (26%). Thus prominence in the organic listings is even more valuable than prominence in the paid listings. And organic listings also enjoy a greater perception of trust than the paid listings because searchers assume that results placed in the organic listings are more authoritative.

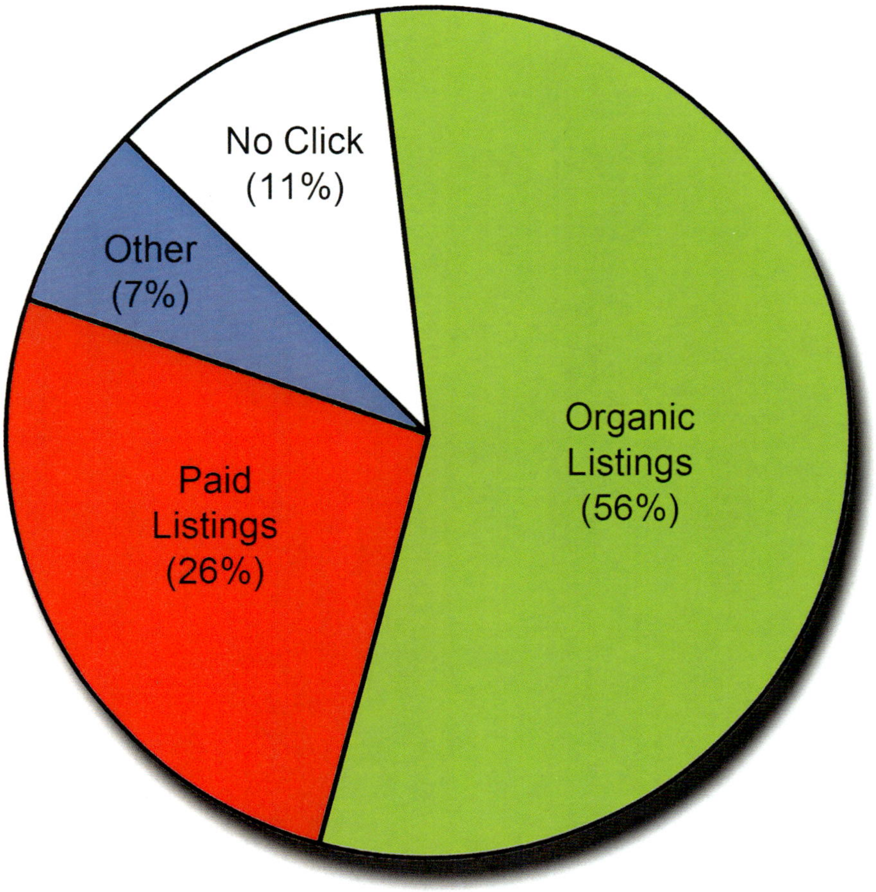

Figure 2 – Distribution of clicks among all types of search results.

Being positioned at the top of these organic listings is particularly valuable because SEO is a contest where the winner takes most of the spoils. The top placed organic listing takes an average of 42% of the organic clicks. Additionally, an average of 15% of organic clicks are taken by the second listing, and 9% are taken by the third listing. Websites listed on the bottom half of the page (in positions six through ten) each receive less than 5% of the organic clicks. Websites listed beyond the first page (in position eleven or higher) each receive less than 1% of the clicks.

If your site is not on the first page, and, in particular, if it is not in the top three positions on the first page, it will not receive much organic traffic from Google. Thus the mission of most SEO campaigns should be to have a site included in the organic listings, and in particular to have a site positioned at the top of the organic listings.

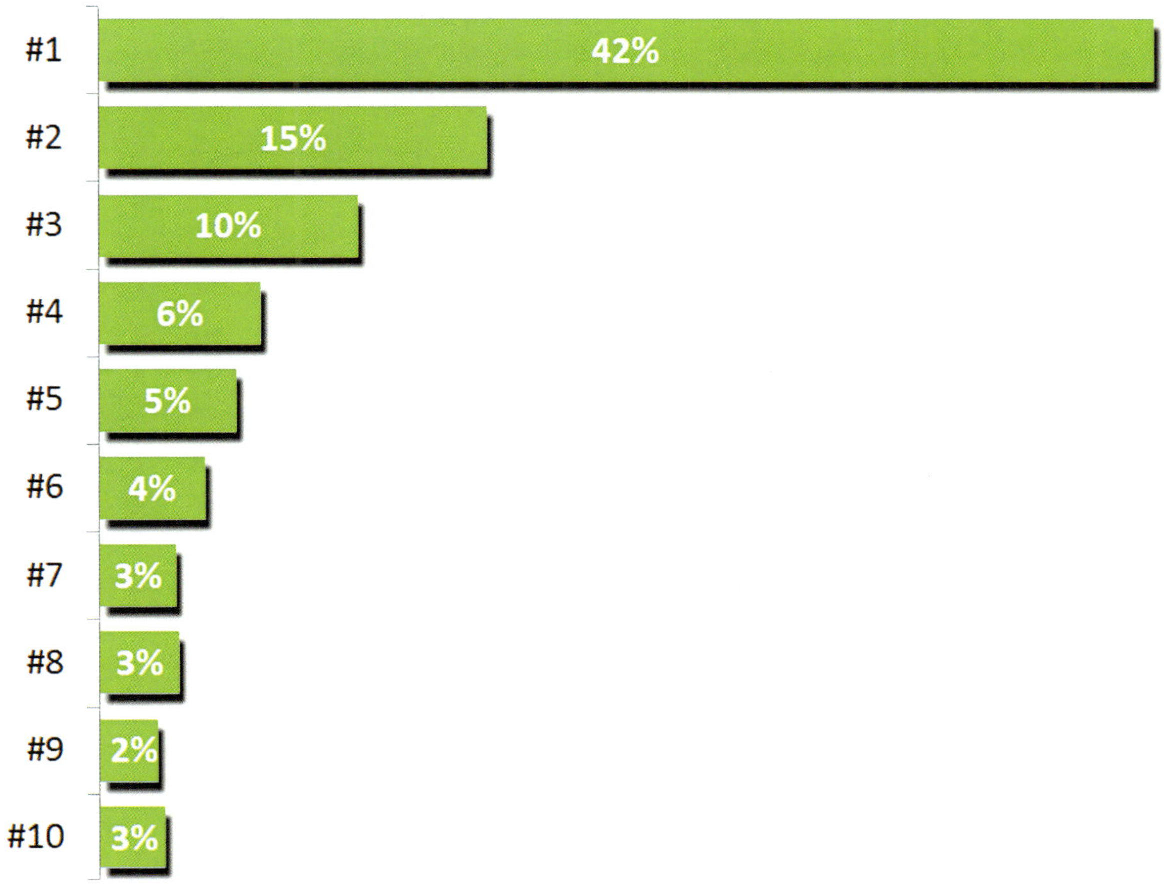

Figure 3 – Distribution of clicks among organic search results by position.

A good SEO campaign has three components:

- **Keyword Strategy** – Determine the keywords to target for your SEO work. Keywords are chosen based on a combination of the likely reward for winning and the amount of work required in winning the keyword. This topic is the focus of this book.
- **On-page Optimization** – Modify your website's pages to make them more attractive to the search engines. On-page optimization includes a collection of techniques such as: creating keyword rich content, interlinking pages, creating a logical internal structure, providing sitemaps for the search engines, and tagging content with machine-readable meta-tags. This topic is addressed in detail in our forthcoming SEO On-Page Optimization book.
- **Off-page Optimization** – Enhance the quantity and quality of your website's connection to the rest of the Internet to signal to the search engines that your site is trusted and relevant in your targeted topics. Off-page optimization is primarily concerned with link building — persuading webmasters of other websites to link to your website. This topic is addressed in detail in our

forthcoming SEO Link Building book. Social media like Twitter, Facebook, and Google+ also play a small but increasing role in off-page optimization.

In an SEO campaign, the keyword strategy work is performed first to identify the targeted keywords. On-page optimization and off-page optimization work begins only after a keyword strategy is completed.

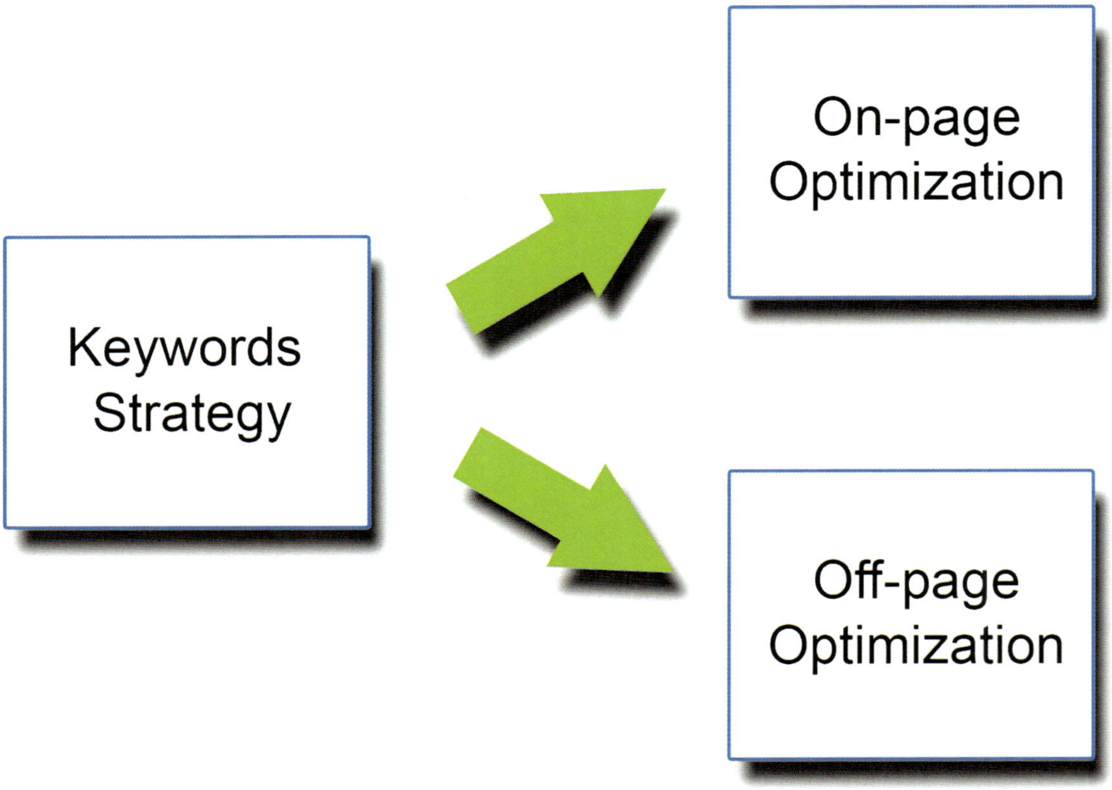

Figure 4 – The three components of an SEO campaign.

Overview of the Keyword Strategy Process

Three steps are necessary to develop a keyword strategy:

Step 1. **Generate Candidate Keywords** – Develop a long list of keywords that might be relevant to your enterprise. At this stage, cast the net broadly to make sure no ideas are missed. Generate candidate keywords through brainstorming, competitor analysis, customer interactions, and automated keyword generation (see Chapter Two).

Step 2. **Analyze Keywords** – Score the keywords across three dimensions:

a. Traffic – the amount of visitors to your site the keywords are likely to generate, taking into account the volume of search traffic and the clickthrough rates (see Chapter Three).

b. Conversion – the amount of profit (or other success metric) that visitors will contribute to your enterprise. This is driven by the rate at which visitors become customers, and the value of each individual customer (see Chapter Four).

c. Competition – the SEO assets of your website benchmarked against competitors to determine the amount of work that will be required to best competitors in the search results (see Chapter Five).

Step 3. **Evaluate Keywords** – Based on the analysis, calculate the payback period for each keyword. Rank the keywords based on their payback period, from best to worst. The best opportunities are selected for Search Engine Optimization (see Chapter Six).

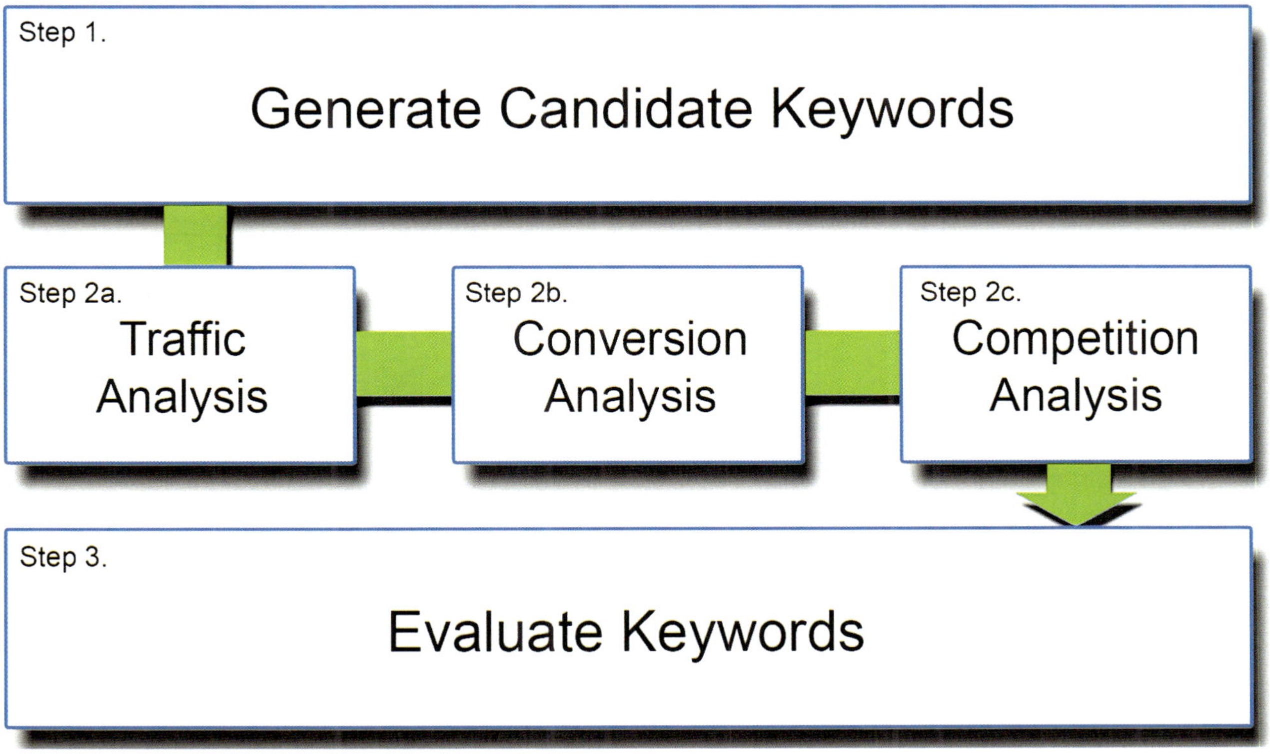

Figure 5 – The keyword strategy process.

SEO Toolbars

To perform the analysis detailed in this book you need two SEO toolbars: the *SEObook toolbar* and the *SEOmoz toolbar*. These free toolbars provide quick access to a wealth of data inside your browser and are to the SEO practitioner what a map and compass are to a soldier.

The toolbars work with recent versions of the Firefox internet browser. If you don't have a recent version of Firefox, download it free from http://www.mozilla.org/. Firefox is the dominant browser among SEO practitioners because it allows the use of plugins that extend the capabilities of the browser (unlike Microsoft Internet Explorer & Apple Safari), and it has a large base of available SEO plugins (unlike Google Chrome).

The SEObook toolbar is available at: http://tools.seobook.com/seo-toolbar/. This toolbar presents a wide array of metrics and is considered the must-have toolbar among SEO practitioners. The toolbar is free, but you will need to register and provide your email address in order to download the toolbar. The toolbar is generously provided by SEObook.com, a site that sells SEO training via subscription ($300 per month). Their training is worth doing, particularly if you are new to SEO. Additionally, support provided by their community to paid subscribers is solid.

The SEOmoz toolbar is available at: http://www.seomoz.org/seo-toolbar. The SEOmoz toolbar provides SEOmoz's own proprietary metrics that are particularly useful for benchmarking competition for a keyword. The free basic toolbar is all you will need for the analysis in this book. A $100/month subscription is required to receive full access to all SEOmoz metrics and link discovery tools. The full service is a must-have for medium to large-scale SEO operations.

Once the two toolbars are installed, your browser will look like this:

Figure 6 – The (A) SEObook toolbar and (B) SEOmoz toolbar.

Use of key metrics displayed on the toolbars is covered in Chapter 5. A quick reference chart is also provided in the back of the book (Appendix 1). For SEO practitioners, interpreting the numbers on these toolbars is important and should become second nature. Look at the numbers every time you navigate to a website and you will begin to develop a feeling for what the numbers mean and how much work is required to change them.

Information Management

Formulating a keyword strategy is a data-intensive exercise, making information management critical. You will perform scores of analyses and generate thousands of data points. Recording and organizing the data helps you keep track of the work that has been done and the work that remains outstanding. Organization also makes the information accessible when you need to refer back to the data for decision support. Keeping a journal of your work allows you to accumulate experience and learn from your mistakes (or bask in the glow of your oracular brilliance).

Record your data on a spreadsheet. We provide a Microsoft Excel spreadsheet template with formulas and annotations at: http://www.seomap.com/seo/keyword-strategy/spreadsheet/.

The spreadsheet is organized into five worksheets:

- **Candidate Keywords** – captures the candidate keywords (Chapter Two).
- **Traffic Analysis** – forecasts the amount of onsite traffic you will experience from each specific keyword as a result of improving your search rank (Chapter Three).
- **Conversion Analysis** – forecasts the value of each new visitor received from a specific keyword (Chapter Four).
- **Competition Analysis** – forecasts the cost of attaining the top ranking for each keyword (Chapter Five).
- **Evaluate Keywords** – forecasts the payback period for your SEO investment for each keyword (Chapter Six).

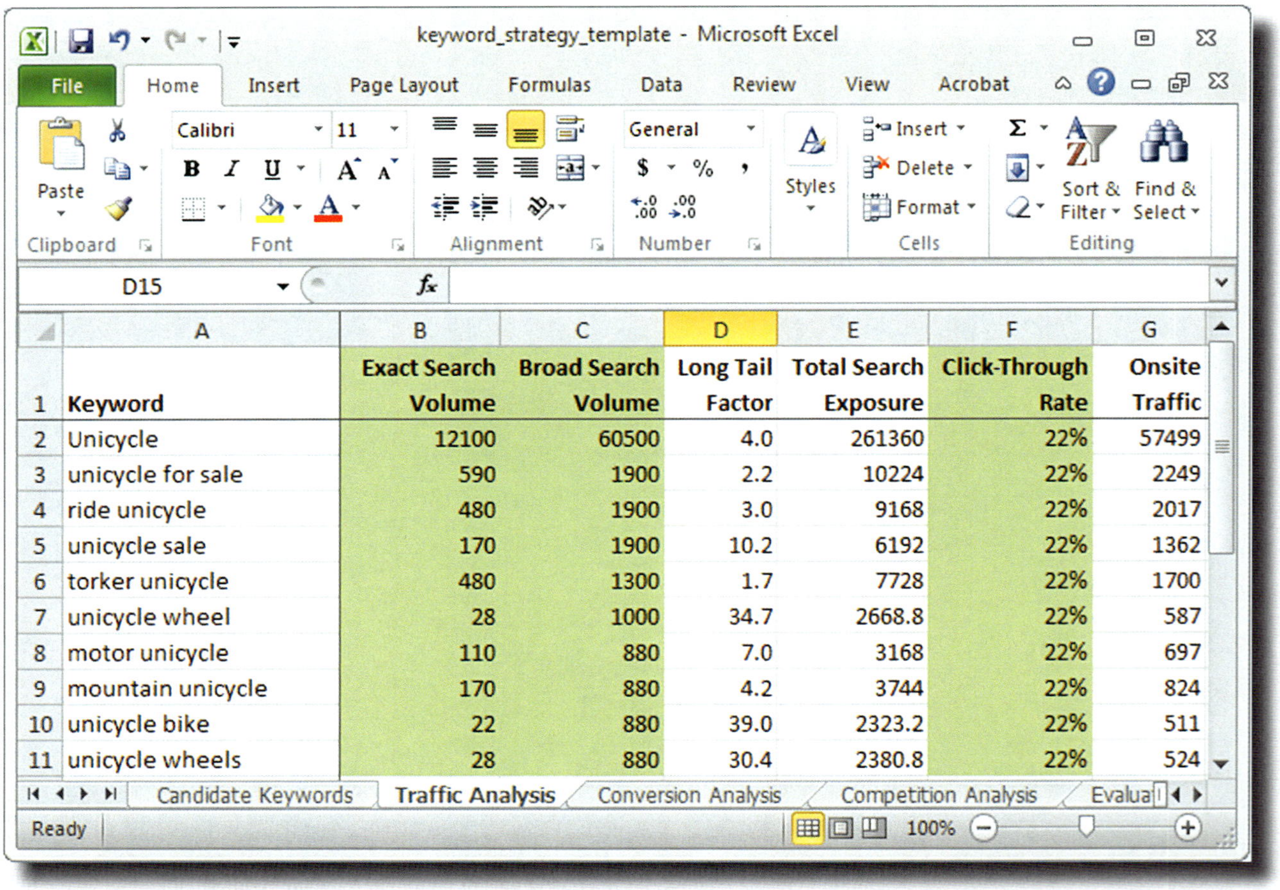

	Keyword	Exact Search Volume	Broad Search Volume	Long Tail Factor	Total Search Exposure	Click-Through Rate	Onsite Traffic
2	Unicycle	12100	60500	4.0	261360	22%	57499
3	unicycle for sale	590	1900	2.2	10224	22%	2249
4	ride unicycle	480	1900	3.0	9168	22%	2017
5	unicycle sale	170	1900	10.2	6192	22%	1362
6	torker unicycle	480	1300	1.7	7728	22%	1700
7	unicycle wheel	28	1000	34.7	2668.8	22%	587
8	motor unicycle	110	880	7.0	3168	22%	697
9	mountain unicycle	170	880	4.2	3744	22%	824
10	unicycle bike	22	880	39.0	2323.2	22%	511
11	unicycle wheels	28	880	30.4	2380.8	22%	524

Figure 7 – Keyword strategy spreadsheet in Microsoft Excel.

2 Candidate Keywords

Summary: Develop a keyword strategy by preparing an exhaustive list of potential keywords. Keywords are generated via:

- **Brainstorming** – Use internal expertise on the product and customer to generate keywords.

- **Competitor Reconnaissance** – Mine competitor websites for keywords leveraging keyword selection work they have already performed.

- **Customer Interactions** – Utilize customer service interactions to find keywords from the voice of the customer.

- **Machine Suggestions** – Supplement the keyword list with computer generated suggestions from the Google Keyword Tool.

"As one gets older one sees many more paths that could be taken. Artists sense within their own work that kind of swelling of possibilities, which may seem a freedom or a confusion."

Jasper Johns, Artist (1930 -).

The first stage in keyword strategy development is to create an exhaustive list of potential keywords. Think broadly to ensure as many candidate keywords as possible are considered. The goal is to not miss any high potential keywords. In the following stages, the keyword list will be winnowed, but at this stage breadth of thought is the most important consideration.

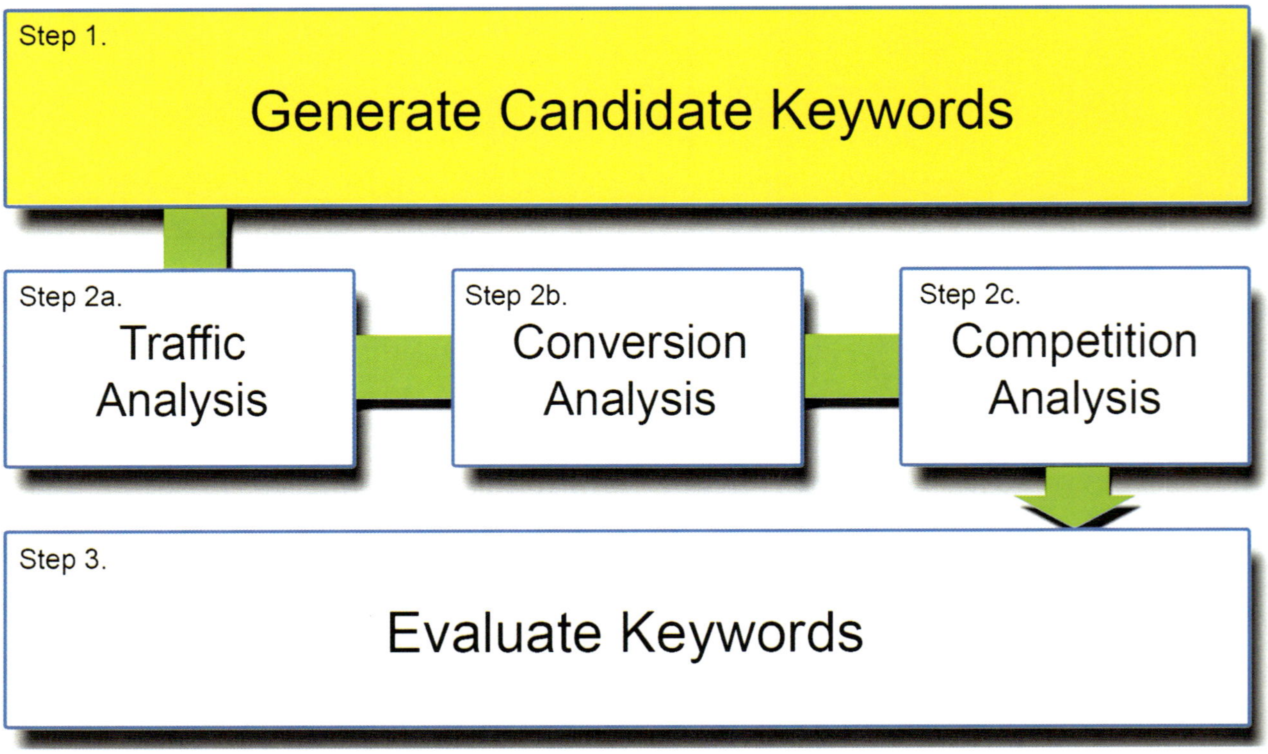

Figure 8 – Generating candidate keywords is the first step of developing a keyword strategy.

Brainstorm Keywords

Keyword strategy begins with brainstorming. Use your knowledge of the product or service, to quickly generate a list of initial keywords. This is a good opportunity to engage the organization, customers, and the general public to receive multiple perspectives. The objective is to generate keywords that your target audience uses, rather than industry jargon. Customer service representatives who answer customer calls and emails tend to be the best calibrated for this task since they have a better understanding of the words that customers use when describing your product or service.

The following three categories of keywords will spur further thinking:

- **Product** – List keywords that directly describe your product or service. Think not only of the official name but also the name of the category and any nicknames. Then think about synonyms. There are usually many different ways to describe a product category. For example, if you sold an organic bug spray you would look at keywords that directly describe the product such as *organic bug spray*. Add synonyms like *mosquito repellent* and *insect spray*. Look at plurals, and other forms of the word, for example, *bug sprays*. And add more specific and more general keywords, such as *natural bug spray* and *bug spray* respectively.

- **Problem** – List keywords that describe the problem that your product or service solves. While many people search directly for a product, a significant segment searches instead for solutions to problems. For example, in regard to a bug spray, investigate problem-based keyword phrases like *stop mosquito bites* and *how to avoid bug bites*.

- **Complement** – Consider keywords that describe complementary topics. For example, to market your bug spray you might target keywords like *mosquito bite treatment* or *bug free gardens*. While providing web users the content they want on treating bug bites, you can find elegant ways to market your bug spray products to them. Although conversion rates tend to be lower for these tangential topics, these keywords may be an opportunity if there is high traffic volume and little competition.

Place the keywords from your brainstorming into the *Keyword* column of the *Candidate Keywords* worksheet.

Competitor Reconnaissance

Competitor reconnaissance is an attempt to learn from competitors' troop placement. We look at where competitors have decided to deploy their SEO resources. When a smart competitor chooses to deploy a lot of their resources to winning a particular keyword, it tells us that they think the keyword is valuable — a good indication that it will be valuable to us as well.

SEO-savvy competitors will have performed at least a rudimentary keyword analysis. In a move of SEO jujitsu, turn their hard work to your advantage. Piggyback on your competitors efforts by examining their webpages and their choice of keywords, adding relevant keywords to your candidate list. Even examining the work of non-SEO-savvy competitors can be useful. While non-SEO-savvy competitors most likely did not perform any keyword analysis, their choice of language and the way they describe their product or service may provide you with additional keyword ideas.

Identify competitors by asking people within the business and by using Google to find websites that rank well for the primary keywords in your niche. Make a deep visit to the competitor sites, and collect data from the homepages and the relevant interior pages.

Review the words that are used on competitor webpages, and examine competitor keyword rankings to discern the keywords that they are targeting. Below, we will discuss each in turn:

Competitor On-Page Keywords

Most sophisticated competitors will use important keywords in the page title, headings, meta-tags, and text of their website. Review competitor websites and look for their use of keywords in those areas.

Step 1: Examine the Page Title

Navigate to the selected page. At the top of your browser, immediately below the menu bar and above the browser window is the webpage title (you can also look at the page source code and search for the words inside the <title> </title> tags). An SEO-savvy competitor will embed keywords in this title, so examine the page titles for a competitor's webpages and extract potentially relevant keywords.

> View page titles at the top of competitors pages.

For example, if you sold office chairs, you would take a look at relevant competitor webpages, such as this one on the HomeDecorators.com website.

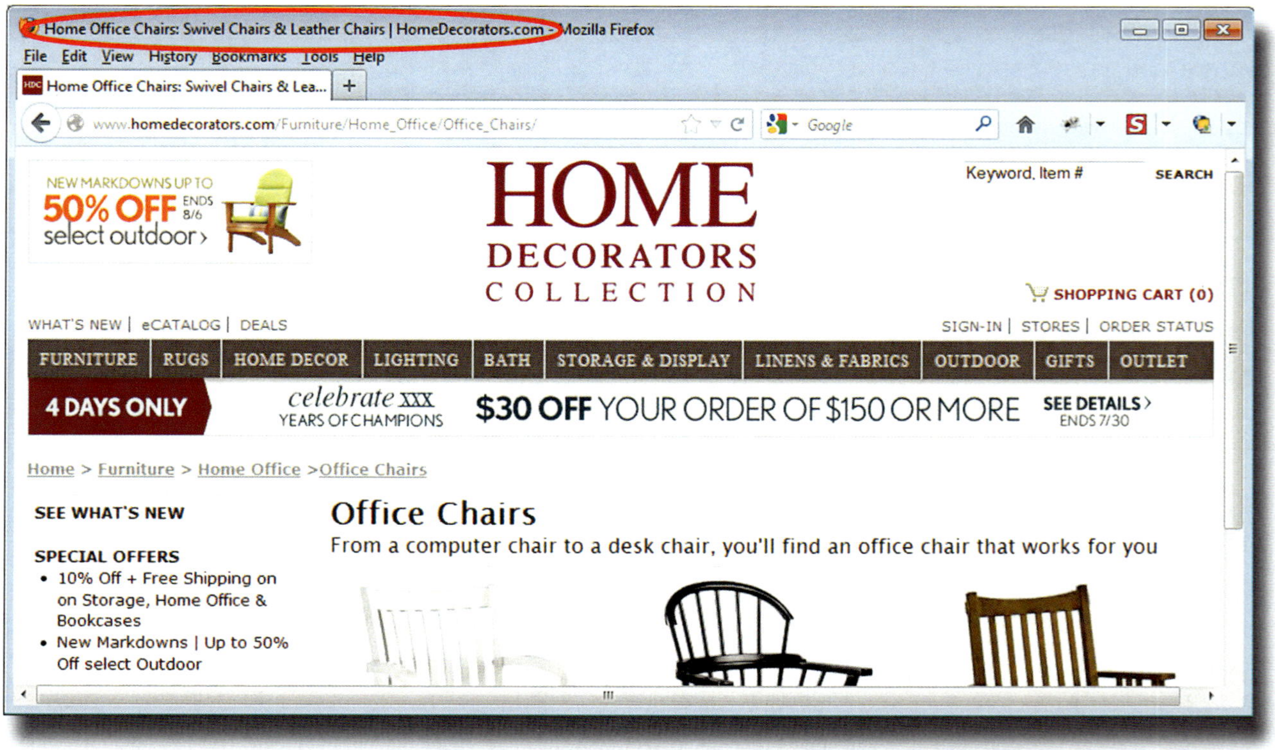

Figure 9 – Examine the titles of competitor webpages for keywords.

The page title is: *Home Office Chairs: Swivel Chairs & Leather Chairs | HomeDecorators.com*. From this, you can surmise that some important keywords in this niche are *office chair(s)*, *swivel chair(s)*, *home office chair(s)*, and *leather chair(s)*. As always, apply a common sense filter when adding keywords. For example, it makes sense that someone looking for an office chair could be searching using the keyword *swivel chair*.

Step 2: Look at Meta-Tags

Meta-tags are code placed in webpages that are not displayed on the website, but are visible to the search engines to help them categorize the website and discern the content.

To view the meta-tags, start by viewing the source code for the page. This is done by right-clicking somewhere on the page and selecting *View Page Source* (or some variant like *View Source* depending on your browser). This opens a browser window that shows html code for the webpage.

> Right click on the page and select *View Page Source*. Then examine the meta-keywords and meta-description.

Note that not all websites use meta-tags. If you can't find the meta-tags on a particular website, it means that the website is not tagging its pages. If this is the case, just move on to the remaining steps.

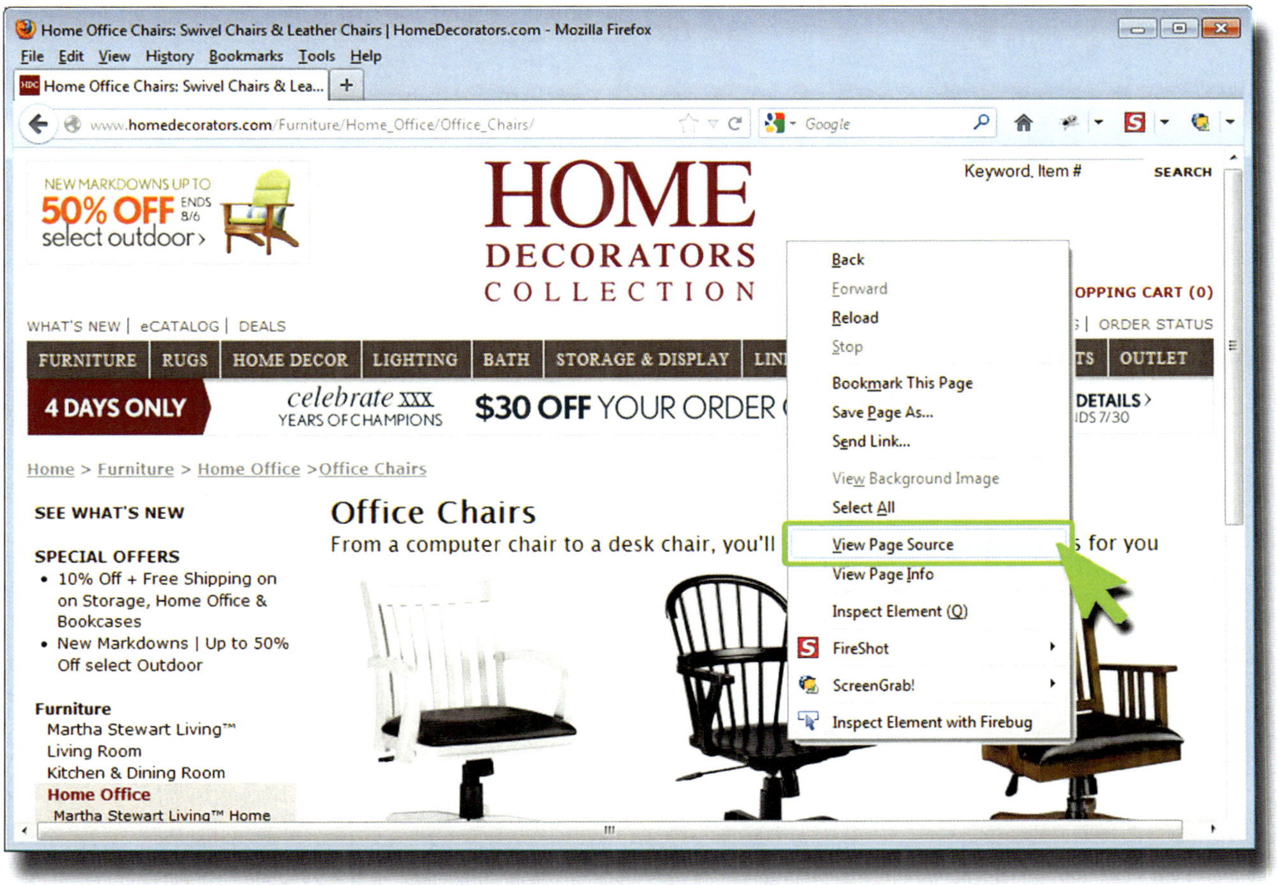

Figure 10 – To view the source code, right click on webpage, and click *View Page Source*.

Keyword Meta-Tags

Keyword meta-tags are found near the top of the page. Keyword meta-tags tell the search engines what the website owner thinks are the primary keywords for the website. Keyword meta-tags are used by some search engines to help classify webpages. Keyword meta-tags are found in code that looks like the following:

<meta name="keywords" contents="keyword1, keyword2, keyword3, etc" />

In our example, the HomeDecorators.com office chairs page, the keyword meta-tags are on the sixth line of the source code. The keyword meta-tags are as follows:

> <meta name="keywords" content="computer chair, desk chair, home office chairs, leather office chair, office chair, office chairs, swivel chair, leather executive chair, leather office chairs" />

This yields: *computer chair(s)*, *desk chair(s)*, *home office chair(s)*, *leather office chair(s)*, *office chair(s)*, *swivel chair(s)*, *leather executive chair(s)*, and *leather office chair(s)*.

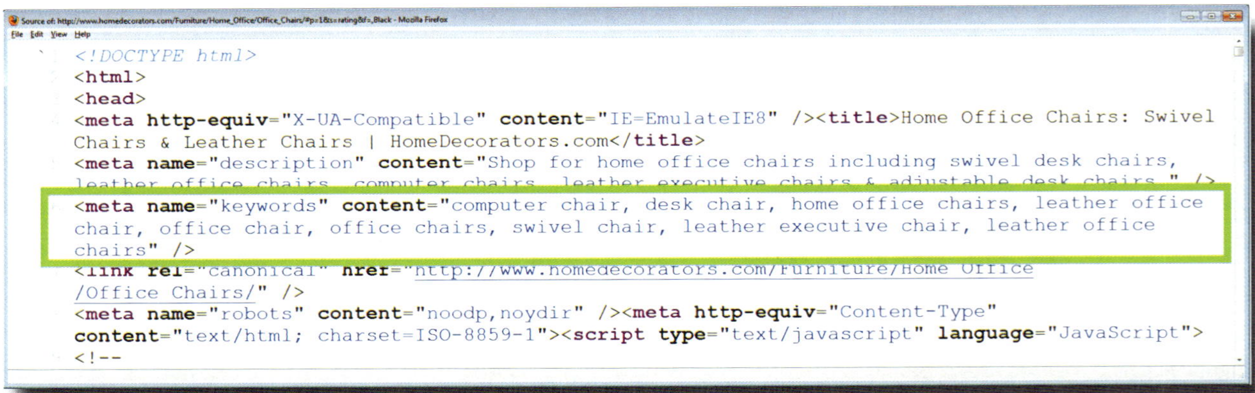
```
<!DOCTYPE html>
<html>
<head>
<meta http-equiv="X-UA-Compatible" content="IE=EmulateIE8" /><title>Home Office Chairs: Swivel
Chairs & Leather Chairs | HomeDecorators.com</title>
<meta name="description" content="Shop for home office chairs including swivel desk chairs,
leather office chairs, computer chairs, leather executive chairs & adjustable desk chairs." />
<meta name="keywords" content="computer chair, desk chair, home office chairs, leather office
chair, office chair, office chairs, swivel chair, leather executive chair, leather office
chairs" />
<link rel="canonical" href="http://www.homedecorators.com/Furniture/Home Office
/Office Chairs/" />
<meta name="robots" content="noodp,noydir" /><meta http-equiv="Content-Type"
content="text/html; charset=ISO-8859-1"><script type="text/javascript" language="JavaScript">
<!--
```

Figure 11 – Keyword Meta-Tags in the webpage source code.

Description Meta-Tag

Close to the keyword meta-tags will be the description meta-tag. The description meta-tag tells the search engines what the website owner wants the search engines to display as the blurb for their webpage when that page appears in the search results. SEO-savvy website owners will write a blurb that is rich in relevant keywords. The code appears in this format:

<meta name="description" contents="An overview of the webpage, usually written in prose. This short description will be rich in keywords relevant to the page." />

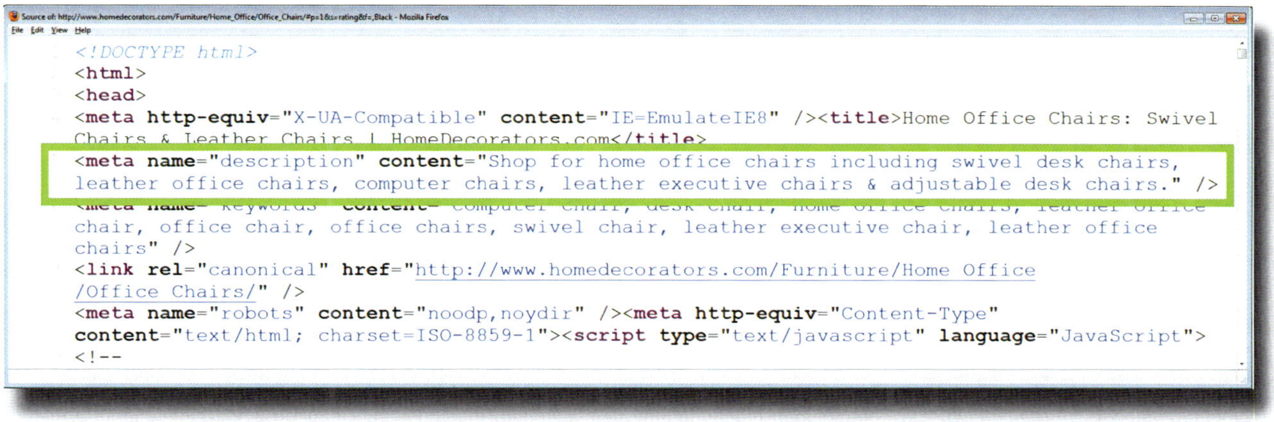

Figure 12 – Description Meta-Tag in the webpage source code.

In our HomeDecorators.com example the description meta-tags are as follows:

> <meta name="description" content="Shop for home office chairs including swivel desk chairs, leather office chairs, computer chairs, leather executive chairs & adjustable desk chairs." />

Thus we can extract the keywords: *home office chair(s)*, *office chair(s)*, *swivel desk chair(s)*, *desk chair(s)*, *leather office chair(s)*, *computer chair(s)*, *leather executive chair(s)*, *executive chair(s)*, and *adjustable desk chair(s)*.

Step 3: Examine Headings

> View page headings on competitors pages.

Examine page headings and subheadings on competitor webpages. SEO-savvy webmasters will embed keywords in these headings. Add these keywords to your *Candidate Keyword* list. Take a moment to pause and thank your competitors for being so thoughtful!

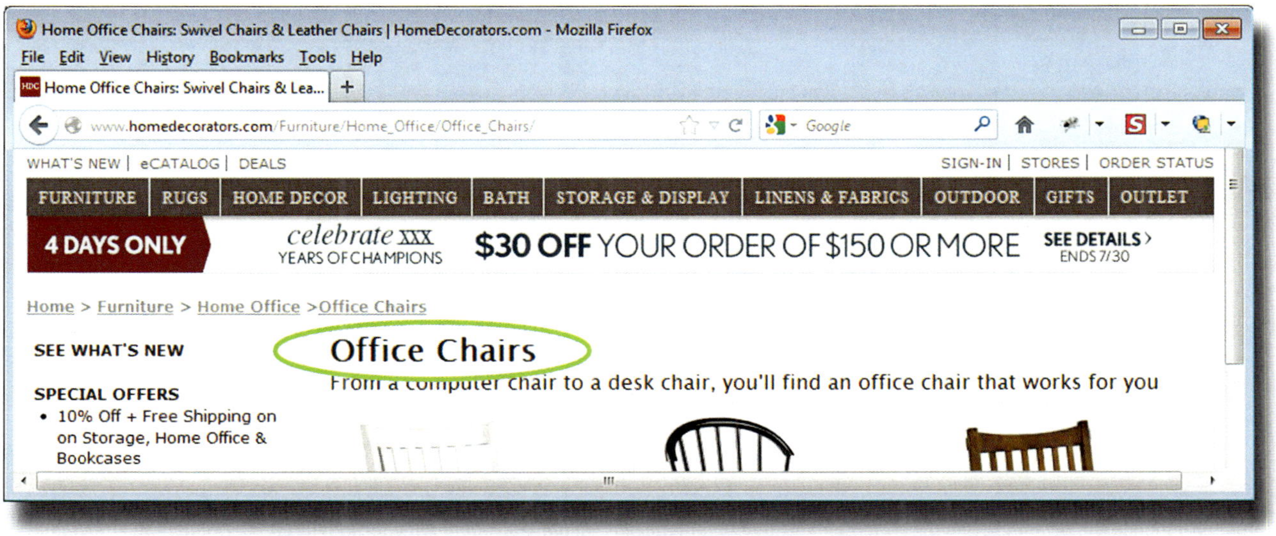

Figure 13 – Examine competitor webpage headings for keywords.

In our example, the page has a single main heading, *Office Chairs*, and no sub-headings. This, of course, gives us the keyword: *Office Chair(s)*.

Step 4: Examine On-Page Text

SEO-savvy competitors will embed keywords in the text, often squirreled away at the bottom of the page.

View on-page text.

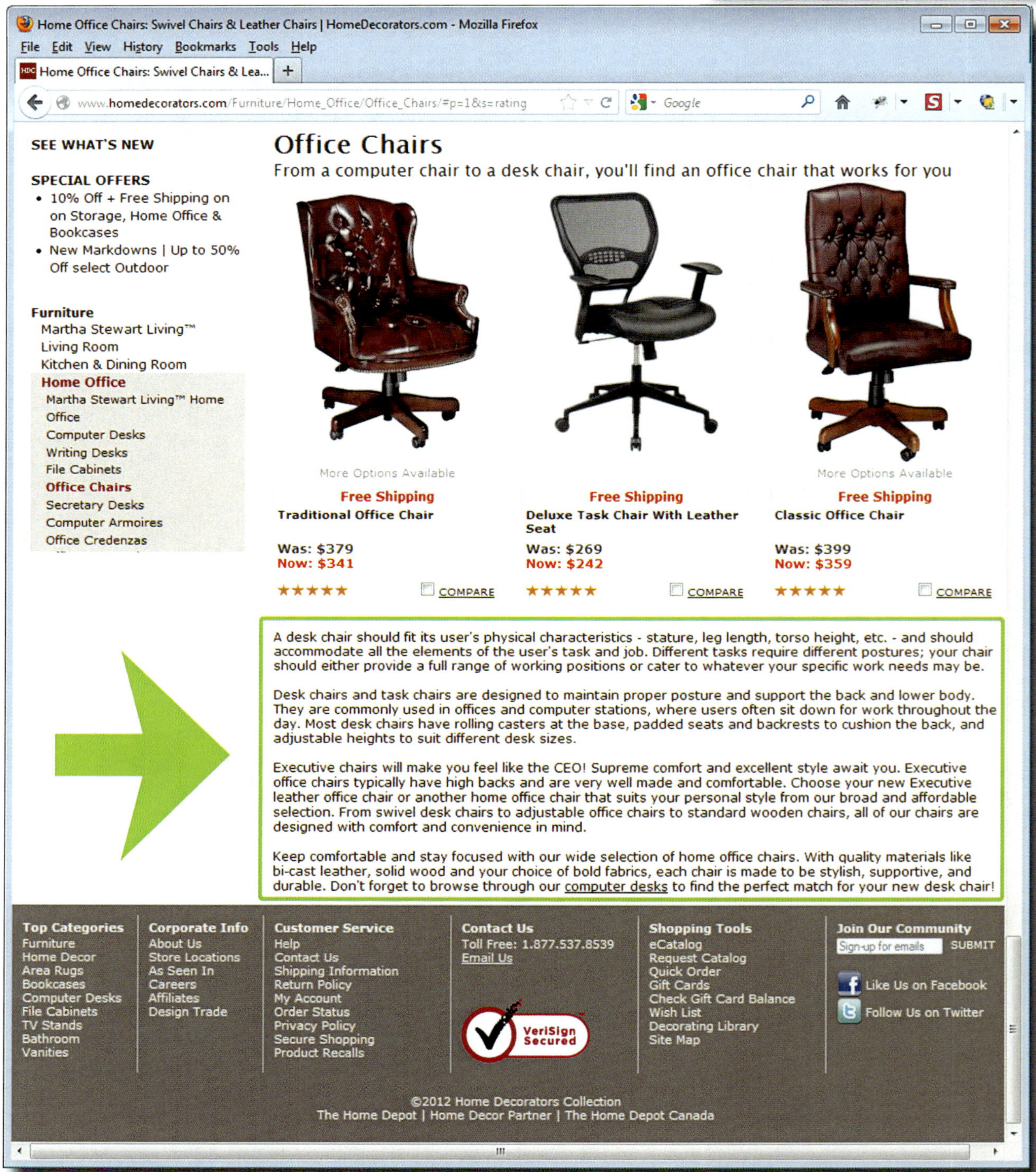

Figure 14 – Examine competitor webpage text for keywords.

In our example the competitor has placed four paragraphs of keyword-rich text at the bottom of the page in an attempt to increase their search traffic:

> *A desk chair should fit its user's physical characteristics - stature, leg length, torso height, etc. - and should accommodate all the elements of the user's task and job. Different tasks require different postures; your chair should either provide a full range of working positions or cater to whatever your specific work needs may be.*
>
> *Desk chairs and task chairs are designed to maintain proper posture and support the back and lower body. They are commonly used in offices and computer stations, where users often sit down for work throughout the day. Most desk chairs have rolling casters at the base, padded seats and backrests to cushion the back, and adjustable heights to suit different desk sizes.*
>
> *Executive chairs will make you feel like the CEO! Supreme comfort and excellent style await you. Executive office chairs typically have high backs and are very well made and comfortable. Choose your new Executive leather office chair or another home office chair that suits your personal style from our broad and affordable selection. From swivel desk chairs to adjustable office chairs to standard wooden chairs, all of our chairs are designed with comfort and convenience in mind.*
>
> *Keep comfortable and stay focused with our wide selection of home office chairs. With quality materials like bi-cast leather, solid wood and your choice of bold fabrics, each chair is made to be stylish, supportive, and durable. Don't forget to browse through our computer desks to find the perfect match for your new desk chair!*

HomeDecorators.com has embedded some keywords in this text to help improve their search rank for these keywords. These keywords include: *desk chair(s)*, *task chair(s)*, *executive chair(s)*, *office chair(s)*, *leather office chair(s)*, *executive leather office chair(s)*, *adjustable office chair(s)*, *wooden chair(s)*, *home office chair(s)*, and *new desk chair(s)*.

After mining your competitor's website for keywords, add these keywords to the *Candidate Keywords* worksheet in the *Keyword* column. Now we turn our attention from the keywords our competitors are targeting to the keywords that our competitors are actually winning in the search engines.

Competitor Rankings

Examine the keywords that your competitor ranks well for in both the free and paid search engine results. If a competitor has invested resources into becoming well ranked for a keyword, or if they are paying for clicks for a keyword, these are likely to be valuable keywords.

Analyze where your competitors rank well using either the SEMRush tool or the Google

Keyword Tool. Of the two, SEMRush is a better tool, but the Google Keyword Tool has the considerable virtue of being free. Directions for using both are provided below.

SEMRush

Organic and paid rankings data is available through the SEMRush.com service. Enter the name of a website and SEMRush generates a list of all significant keywords for which the competitor ranks well in both organic and paid listings (for Google). The free version of the service gives you the top five keywords, and the paid version ($80 for one-month, $70 per month if you subscribe) reports all significant keywords. For each keyword, you are given information on the site's rank, the volume of searches, and the estimated cost to purchase traffic for the keyword.

Step 1: Enter Competitor's Website

Navigate to http://www.SEMRush.com. Enter the name of a website into the search bar at the top of the page. Select the appropriate country, then click *Search*.

Navigate to SEMRush.com, enter website & click *Search*.

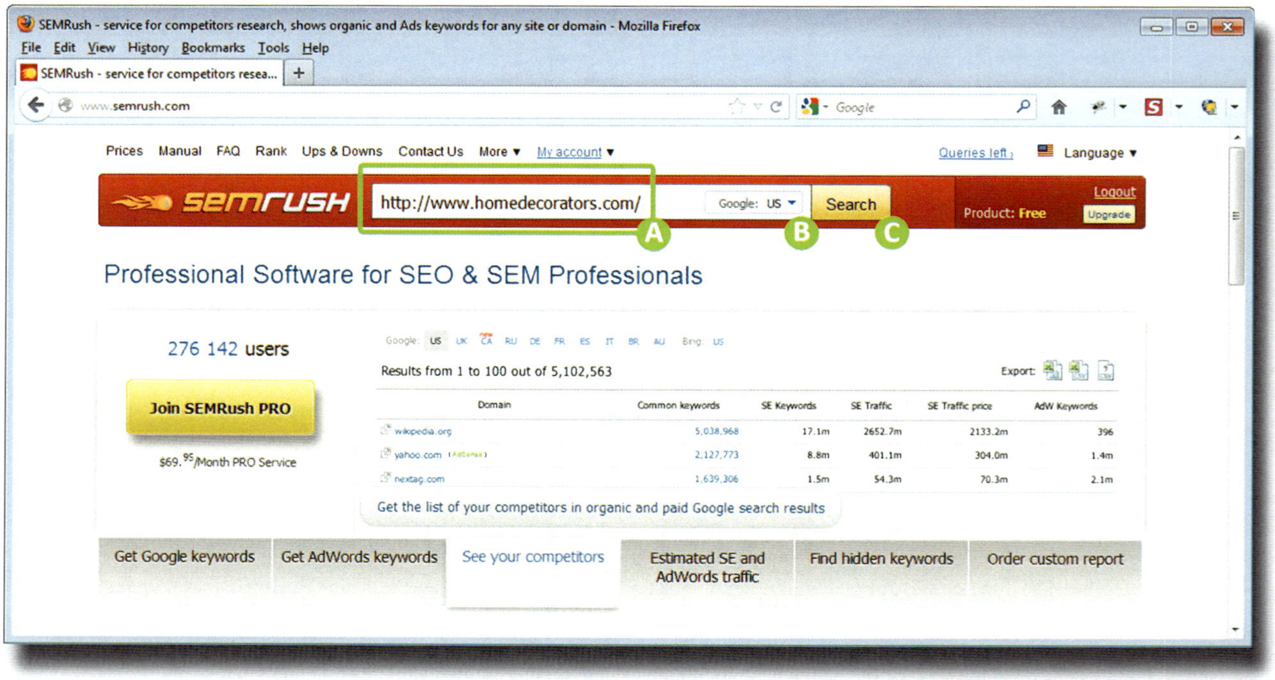

Figure 15 – (A) enter the competitor's website in the SEMRush search bar. (B) select the appropriate country, and (C) click *Search*.

Step 2: Download Data

Export the data for both *Organic Keywords* and *Ads Keywords* by clicking the respective Excel icons. This downloads the full report in Microsoft Excel format.

Click Excel icons to export Organic & Paid Keyword lists

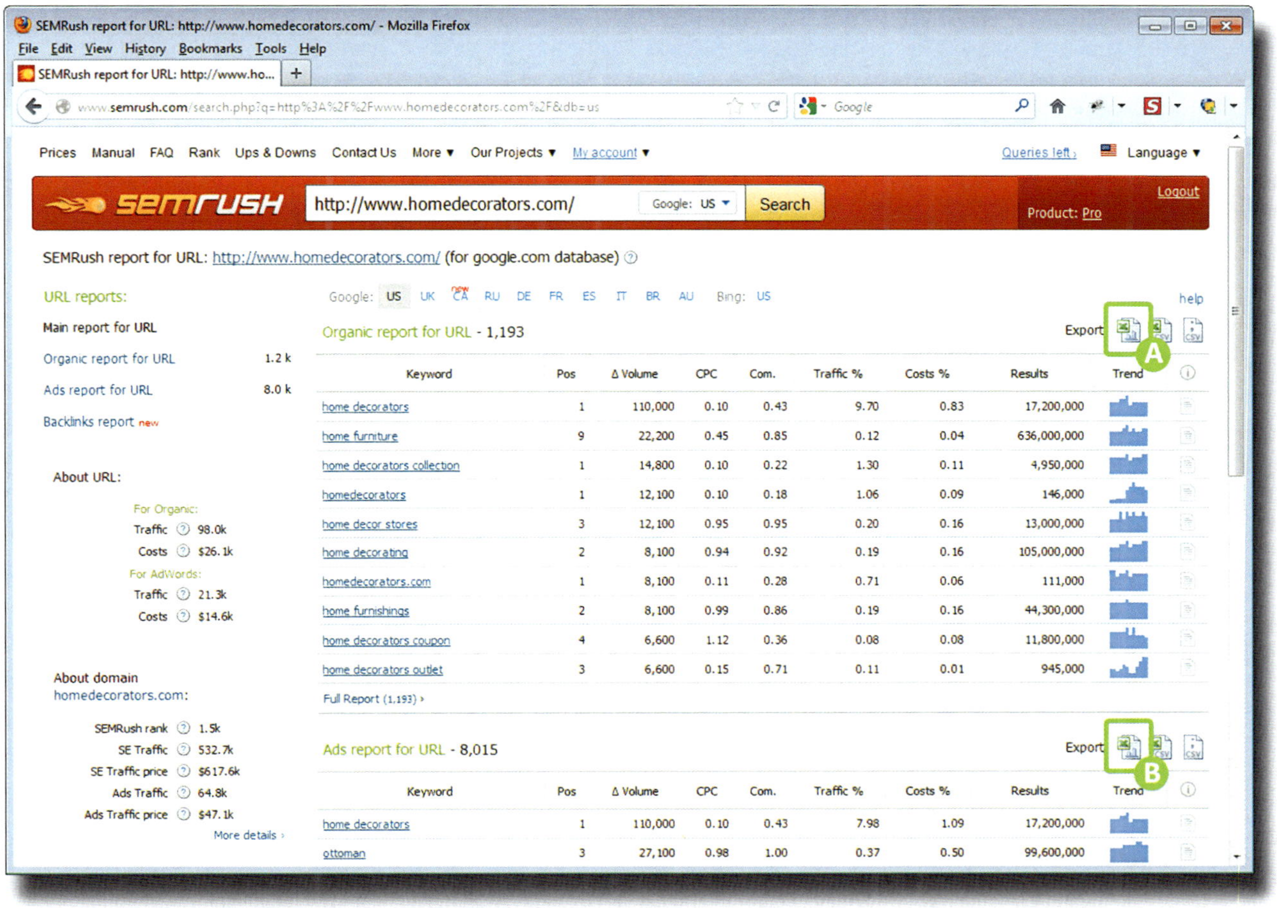

Figure 16 – Download the SEMRush results by clicking the Excel icons for (A) organic keywords, and (B) paid ad keywords.

Step 3: Interpret Data

> Add keywords with significant volume and value to the list.

The data contains a list of keywords the competitor is either ranked for in search, or is paying for using Pay-Per-Click advertising. For each keyword, SEMRush displays:

- **Position** – the Google Search Rank Position of the competitor's website for the keyword for the selected country
- **Volume** – the monthly traffic volume for exact match for the keyword for the selected country
- **CPC** (Cost-Per-Click) – the average cost to purchase the top paid listing for the keyword in Google AdWords for the selected country

If a competitor is paying a high amount for a click on a keyword, it is likely that either the keyword converts very well or the customers the keyword attracts are highly profitable. Most competitors bid on keywords somewhat rationally and the market is relatively efficient, so if they are willing to more for a first keyword than a second keyword, it is a good indicator that the first keyword is more profitable than the second. Conversely, if there are keywords where the pay-per-click numbers are low (i.e., below $1), it is usually a good indicator that the keywords do not convert well.

	Keyword	Position	Search Volume	CPC	Competition	Traffic (%)	Traffic Cost (%)
2	home decorators	1	110,000	$0.10	0.28	9.48%	0.83%
3	home decorators collection	1	14,800	$0.10	0.16	1.27%	0.11%
4	decorating	20	14,800	$0.86	0.33	0.00%	0.00%
5	homedecorators	1	14,800	$0.10	0.16	1.27%	0.11%
6	home decor stores	3	12,100	$0.97	0.92	0.19%	0.17%
7	home decorating	2	9,900	$0.95	0.86	0.23%	0.19%
8	homedecorators.com	1	8,100	$0.12	0.36	0.69%	0.07%
9	home decorators outlet	5	8,100	$0.15	0.4	0.07%	0.00%
10	home furnishings	2	8,100	$1.02	0.83	0.19%	0.17%
11	home decorators coupon	7	5,400	$1.44	0.35	0.03%	0.05%
12	home decorations	2	5,400	$0.88	0.92	0.12%	0.10%
13	home decor catalogs	6	5,400	$0.97	0.92	0.04%	0.04%
14	home decorator	1	3,600	$0.16	0.5	0.31%	0.04%
15	home depot rugs	7	3,600	$0.39	0.88	0.02%	0.00%

Figure 17 – SEMRush results downloaded into Excel.

Using the volume data, Cost-Per-Click data, and common sense, collect the most promising keywords and add them to the *Keywords* column of the *Candidate Keywords* worksheet. (Download a template spreadsheet from our site at: http://www.seomap.com/seo/keyword-strategy/spreadsheet/).

Repeat these three steps for each competitor website.

Google Keyword Tool

A free alternative to SEMRush is the Google AdWords Tool. The Google tool is not as good as SEMRush at identifying lower traffic keywords, but it does a reasonable job of identifying higher traffic keywords.

Step 1: Navigate to the Google Keyword Tool

Go to http://adwords.google.com. You will need to have a Google account and be logged in to continue. Once logged in, click *Tools & Analysis* ⇨ *Keyword Tool*.

Go to adwords.google.com.
Click *Tools & Analysis* ⇨
Keyword Tool.

Step 2: Enter Competitor Website

Enter site in *Website* box. Check *Only show closely related terms*. Set *Advanced Options*. Click *Search*.

Enter the name of the relevant website in the *Website* box. Click the *Only show ideas closely related to my search* checkbox. Check to make sure that *Advanced Options* are set to your target *Location* and *Language* (for most of our readers that is *United States* and *English* respectively), and check that *Devices* is set to *Desktop and laptops*. Finally, click *Search* to get your results.

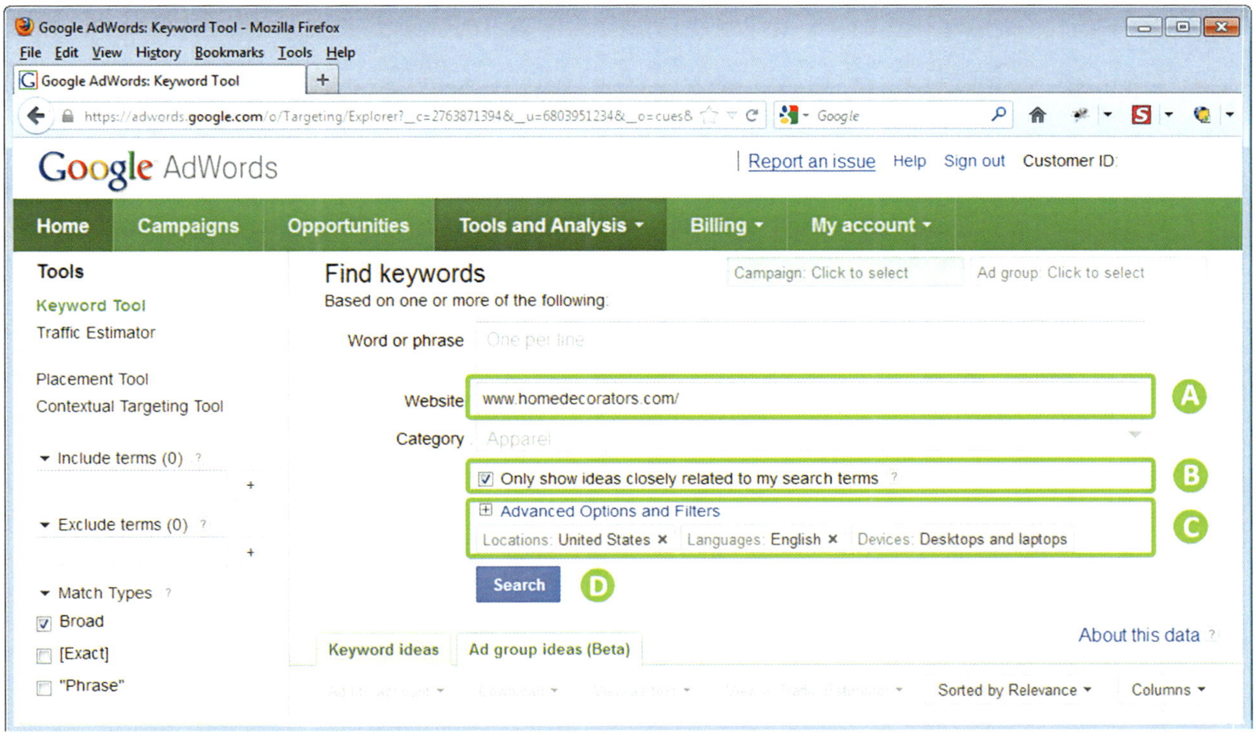

Figure 18 – (A) enter the competitor's webpage in the *Website* box.
(B) Click *Only show idea closely related to my search*.
(C) Select your *Location* and *Language*.
Set devices to *Desktop and laptops*.
(D) Click *Search*.

Step 3: Collect Data

Click *Download* ⇨ *All Search Results*. Add relevant keywords to list.

Results are displayed on-screen. Click *Download* ⇨ *All Search Results*, and select *CSV for Excel* to download the data into a spreadsheet. Triage results, culling keywords which are obviously not a good fit. Add the remaining keywords to the *Candidate Keywords* worksheet in the *Keyword* column of your keyword strategy spreadsheet.

Repeat these steps for each competitor website of interest.

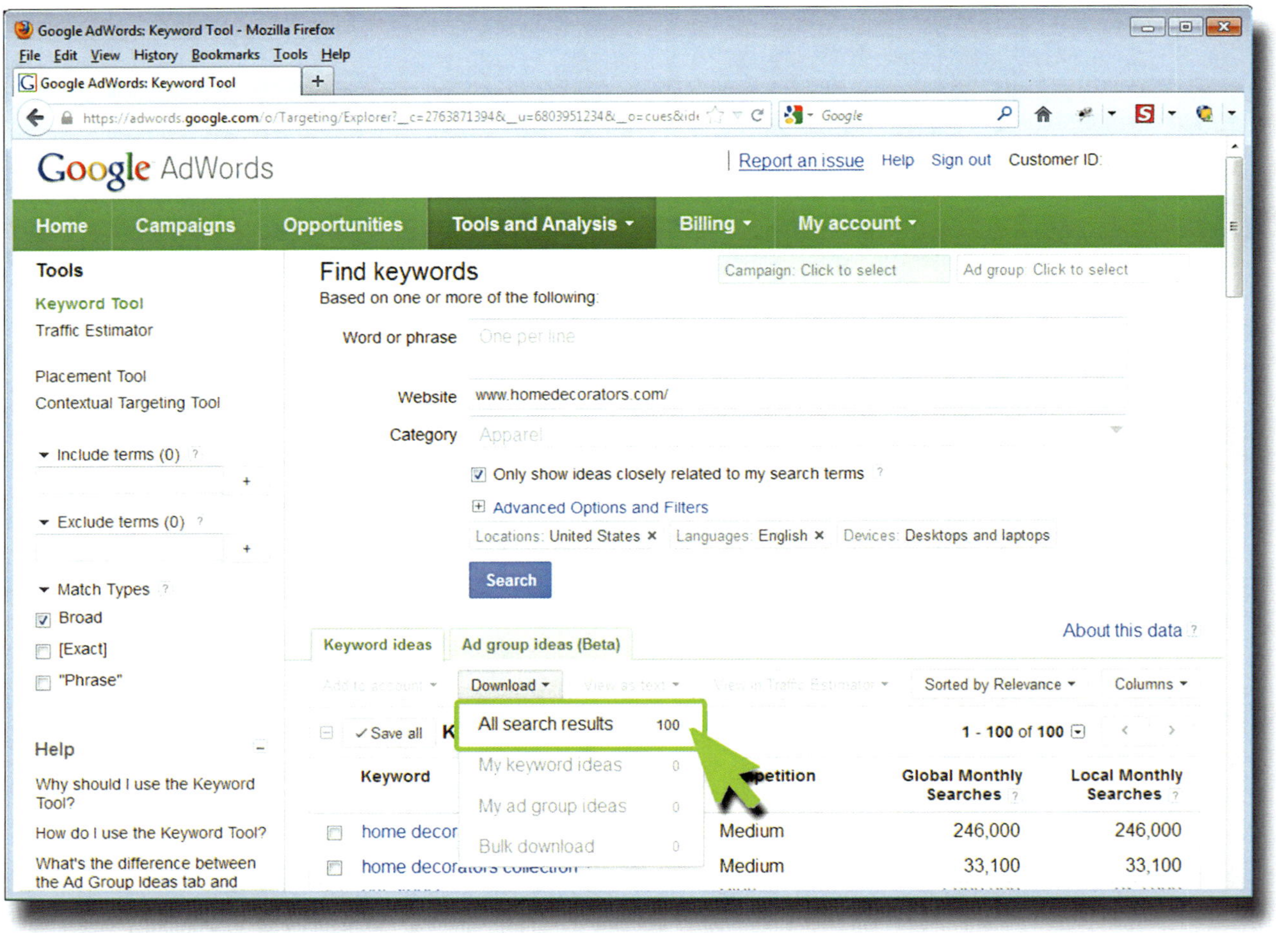

Figure 19 – Download the Google Keyword Tool data by clicking *Download* ⇨ *All search results*.

Competing With Brands?

Many large competitors receive a significant amount of their traffic from keywords related to their brand. For example, a large amount of Gap's website traffic comes from searches related to the Gap brand and not generic clothing terms such as *pants*. So include relevant brand names in your keyword analysis.

When competing in brand conscious segments, optimize for those brand keywords. Although winning branded keywords is unlikely, it is often relatively easy to become the second or third result, where you can promote yourself as being an alternative to the brand. For example, you might create a page comparing your products to those at Gap to capitalize on some of their traffic.

Customer Interactions

Customers are a good source of unconventional keywords. Because they are less familiar with your products, customers often use different words and phrases. This can be a rich vein for mining keywords. Below are a few ideas on how to get keyword insights from customers.

- **Customer Service Representatives** – Customer service representatives who answer customer emails and phone calls are, as we previously mentioned, a great source of keyword ideas. Because they interact daily with customers, they are well calibrated to the word choices that a customer is likely to use when searching for a product.

- **Customer Comments** – Find keyword insights by browsing the customer comments on your own site and the customer comments on competitor sites.

- **Search Box** – If your website has a search function, the search data is usually logged (and if it is not, install one of the many plugins or software packages that will log the data). Browse the logged search queries and look for frequently used search phrases.

- **Forums** – If your industry or product are served by any online forums, visit these forums and observe the language that participants, particularly new participants, use to describe the product.

Once again, add the keywords you generate to the *Candidate Keywords* worksheet in the *Keywords* column.

Machine Suggestions

Once an initial group of keywords is identified the Google Keyword Tool can help you find similar keywords. The keyword tool can also be used as a final check to make sure significant keywords are not overlooked.

Step 1: Navigate to Google Keyword Tool

Go to the Google Keyword Tool (http://adwords.google.com, then click *Tools & Analysis* ⇨ *Keyword Tool*).

> Go to adwords.google.com. Click *Tools & Analysis* ⇨ *Keyword Tool*.

Step 2: Enter Starting Keyword Set

Paste the list of keywords into the *Word or phrase* box. Click the *Only show ideas closely related to my search* checkbox. Ensure *Advanced Options* are set to your target *Location* and *Language* (for most of our readers that is *United States* and *English* respectively), and check that *Devices* is set to *Desktop and laptops*. Then click *Search* to get a list of machine generated candidates.

> Enter keywords in *Word or phrase* box. Check *Only show closely related terms*. Set *Advanced Options*. Click *Search*.

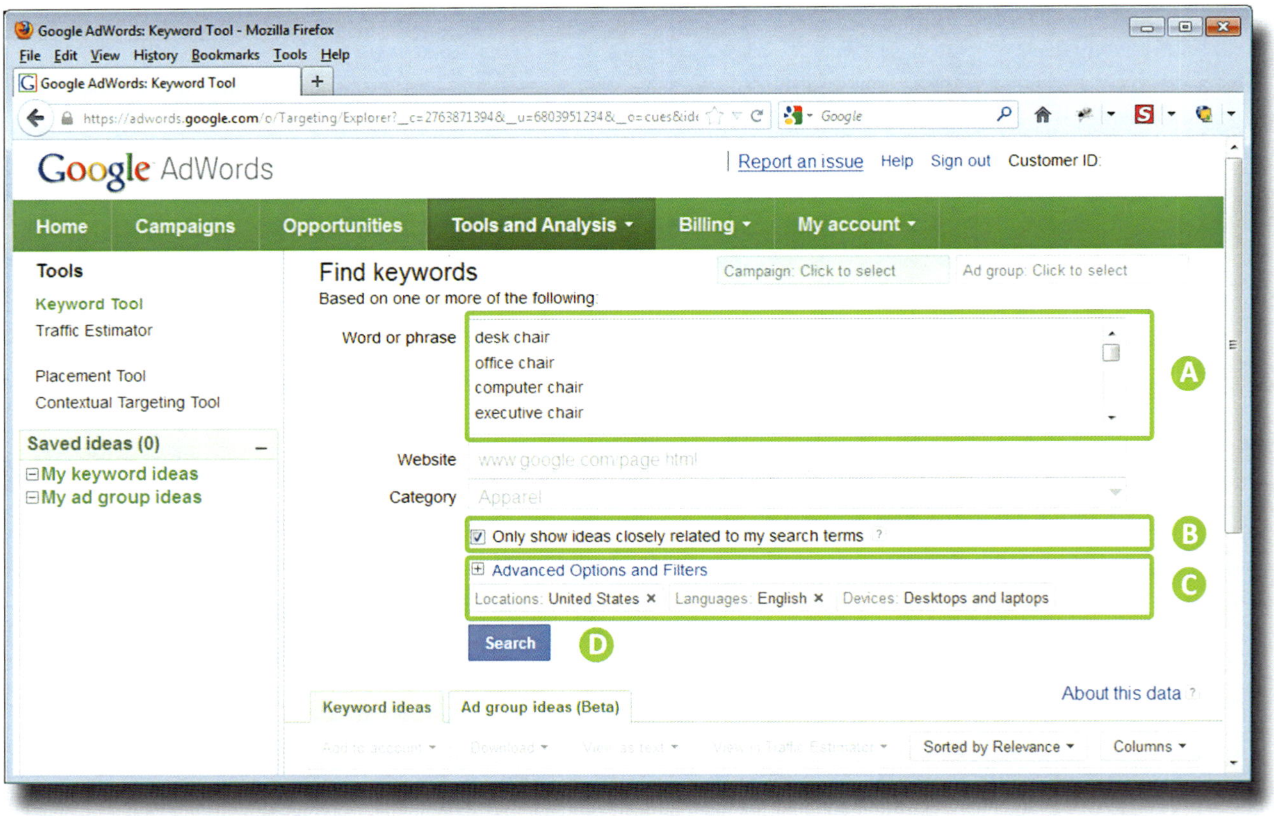

Figure 20 – (A) Enter your preliminary keyword list in the *Word or phrase* box.
(B) Click *Only show ideas closely related to my search*.
(C) Select your *Location* and *Language*.
Set devices to *Desktop and laptops*.
(D) Click *Search*.

Step 3: Collect and Curate Suggested Keywords

Capture this keyword list by clicking *Download* ⇨ *All Search Results*, and selecting *CSV for Excel* to download the data into a spreadsheet.

> Click *Download* ⇨ *All Search Results*. Add relevant keywords to list.

The results you get from the keyword tool need to be manually curated because they often contain irrelevant keywords. Edit the list of suggestions and discard those that are too far afield to be helpful. Add the remaining relevant keywords to the *Candidate Keywords* worksheet of your spreadsheet in the *Keyword* column.

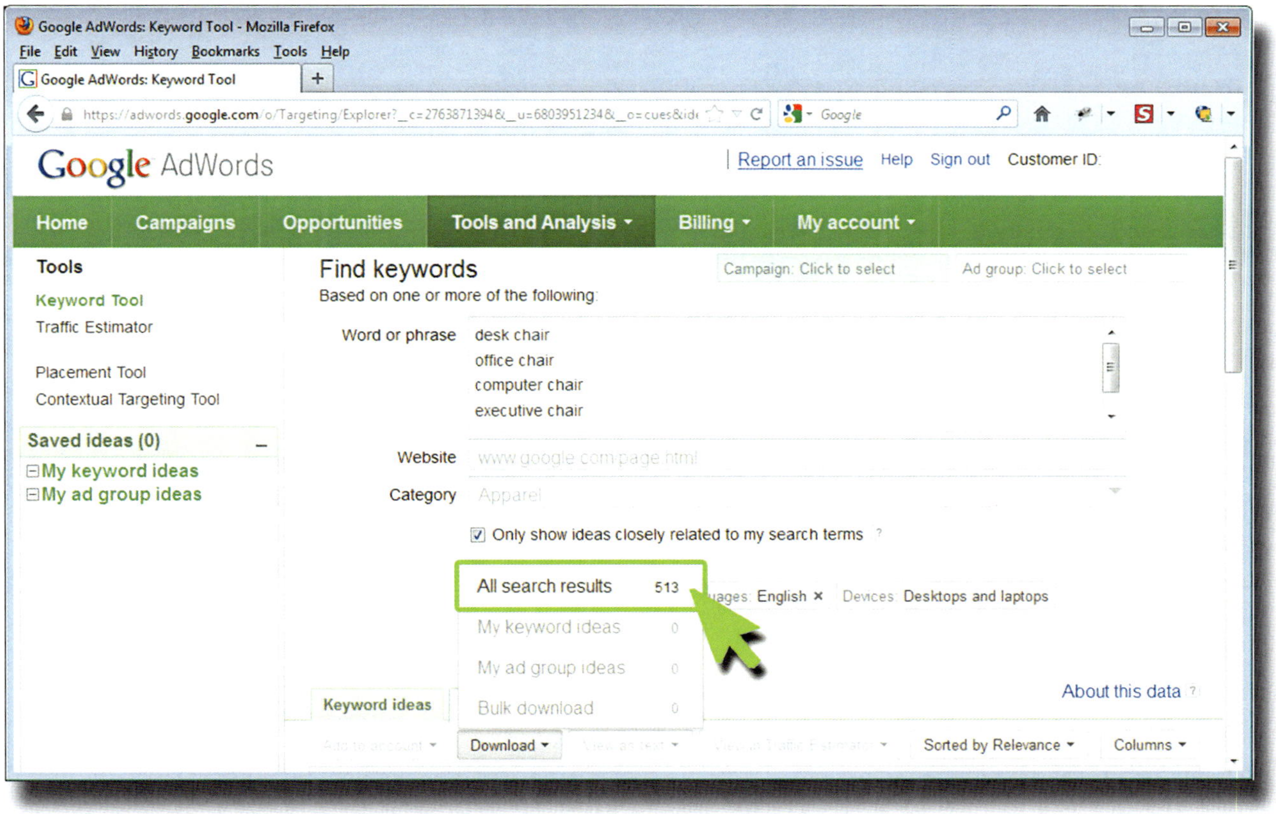

Figure 21 – Download the Google Keyword Tool data, by clicking *Download ⇨ All search results*.

Candidate List

> Remove duplicates in Excel by clicking *Data ⇨ Filter ⇨ Advanced Filter.*

After using the above techniques to identify candidate keywords, consolidate the results in the *Candidate Keywords* worksheet. There will likely be many duplicates in your list, so de-dupe the list. This can be done in Microsoft Excel.

Click your mouse on the top item in the list and drag down until the entire list is selected. Go to the top menu and Select *Data ⇨ Filter ⇨ Advanced Filter*. Click the check box *Unique records only*, then click *OK*. This filter will hide duplicates, irrespective of capitalization. So if *Chair* and *chair* appear in the original list, one will be hidden after the filter is run.

Copy the filtered list and paste it into the *Keywords* column in the *Traffic Analysis* worksheet. You are now ready to begin your keyword analysis.

In the next three chapters we analyze the keywords to determine which keywords are worth pursuing and which keywords should be deprioritized. We begin by looking at traffic data.

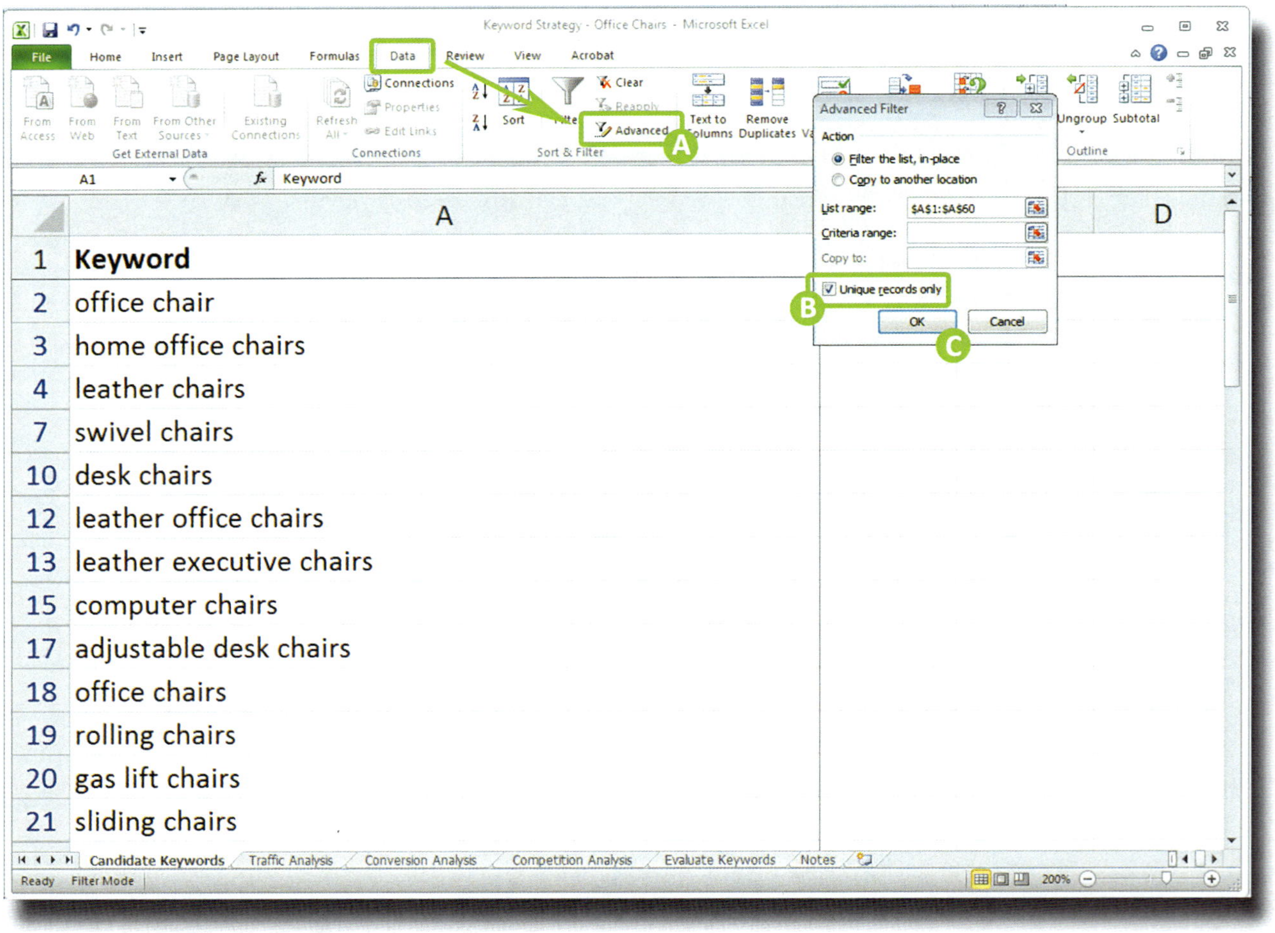

Figure 22 – Filter keyword to remove duplicates

(A) *Data* ⇨ *Filter* ⇨ *Advanced Filter*.

(B) Check *Unique Records only*.

(C) Click *OK*.

3 Traffic Analysis

Summary: Begin the keyword analysis by examining the traffic data associated with the keywords. Traffic will be analyzed across five dimensions:

- **Volume** – The number of internet users that search for individual keywords.
- **Long Tail** – The degree to which searches are concentrated in an exact keyword phrase versus scattered across variations of the keyword phrase.
- **Click-Through** – The rate at which searchers exposed to your search listing click on the listing and visit your site.
- **Trends** – The temporal distribution of visitors and the drivers of this distribution.
- **Strategic Importance** – The keyword's importance to the business beyond the metrics.

Combining this data, you can forecast the number of visitors you will see as a result of achieving a top ranking for each keyword.

"Go fishing where the fish are."
Marketing proverb (unknown).

Traffic analysis tells you how many visitors you are likely to gain as a result of winning specific keywords in the search engines. At the end of this chapter you should have estimates for the amount of traffic that will be associated with winning each keyword.

Begin by looking at the number of searches that are performed for the keywords under consideration and examining both searches for the exact keyword as well as long tail searches. Then, use click-through data to predict the fraction of searches that will click on your search listing and reach your website. Finally, look at traffic trends and strategic considerations that provide insight beyond the data.

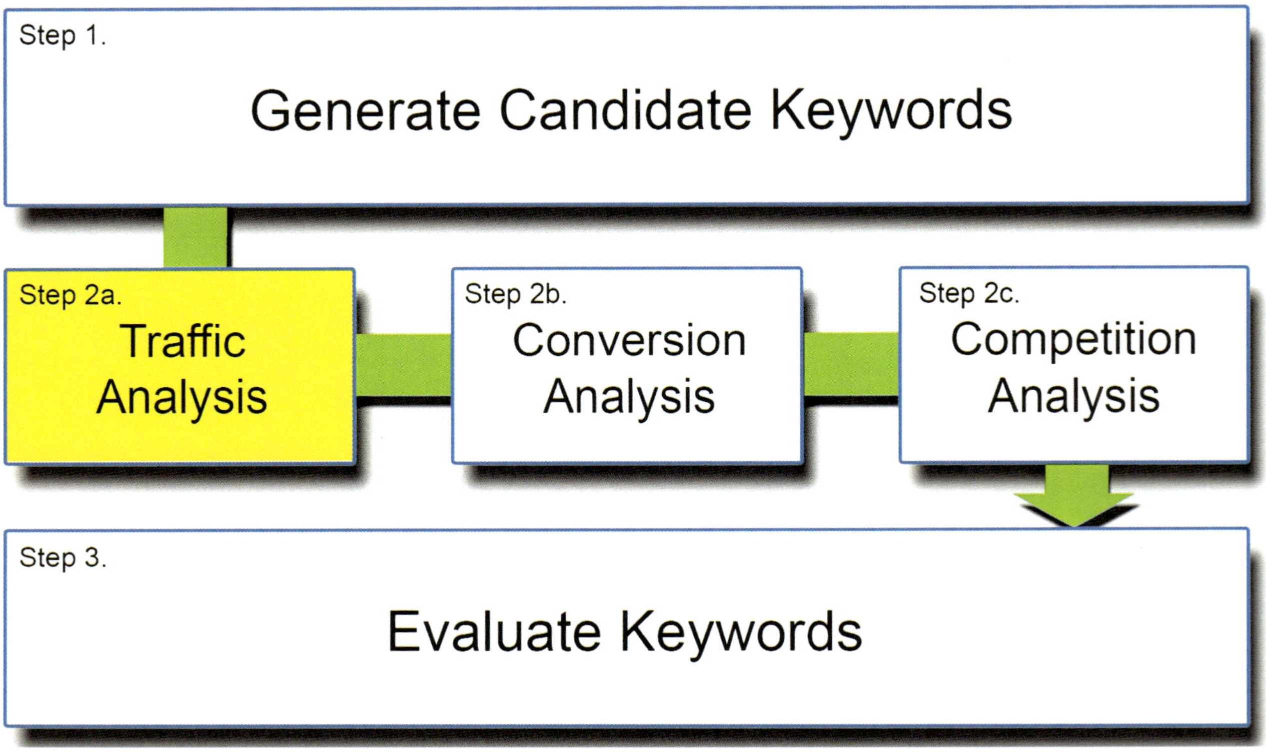

Figure 23 – Traffic analysis is step 2a of developing a keyword strategy.

Traffic Volume

An estimate of the number of searches performed using any keyword can be obtained from the Google Keyword Tool. This tool provides the number of monthly Google searches for each keyword.

Step 1: Navigate to Google Keyword Tool

Go to the Google Keyword Tool (http://adwords.google.com, then click *Tools & Analysis* ⇨ *Keyword Tool*). You will need to have a Google account to use the full version of this tool. The free tool provides data directly from Google, displaying the amount of traffic for any keyword selected, as well as other useful traffic metrics.

> Go to adwords.google.com.
> Click *Tools & Analysis* ⇨ *Keyword Tool.*

Step 2: Select Match Types

Select *Match Types* checkboxes for *Broad* and *[Exact].*

> Select *Match Type* checkboxes for *Broad* and *[Exact].*

Exact match displays searches for the keyword exactly as entered. An exact search for *silk slippers* would give the number of monthly searches for someone that typed in the exact phrase *silk slippers* with no additional words. *Exact match* numbers are useful because they are a good indication of the number of searches a site is exposed to if that site wins a specific keyword. Exact match search data does not, however, account for all the long tail traffic.

Broad match displays the number of searches from any variation on our keywords. For example, a broad search for *silk slippers* would include *silk bedtime slippers*, *slippers made of silk*, *silken slippers* and even *yellow silk slippers size 8 made in Japan under $40.* Collectively these variations, often referred to as *long tail*, represent the vast majority of searches. While each of these individual variations represents a small amount of traffic, collectively the number of long tail searches greatly exceeds the number of searches for the primary keyword. For example, the long tail for *silk slippers* has four times more search volume than the primary keyword, *silk slippers.*

Broad match numbers are useful data points because they provide the aggregate number of searches for the exact keyword and long tail variations. When you optimize for the primary keyword, you often end up ranking well for the associated long tail keywords without any additional effort. For example, if you did an SEO campaign for the keyword *silk slippers* and you subsequently ranked well for that phrase, you would probably rank well for *yellow silk slippers* without needing to put in much extra effort.

There is also an option for *phrase match*, which selects all searches with the phrase, *silk slippers* where the words are contained in that exact order with no words in between. For example, phrase match would pick up *yellow silk slippers made in Japan* but not *silk lined slippers* because in the latter search the words *silk* and *slippers* were separated. This feature generally does not add much value to the analysis. However, *phrase match* is useful as an alternative to *broad match*, where *broad match* is picking up a high volume of extraneous terms that should not be counted.

Step 3: Configure Advanced Options

Click *Advanced Options and Filter*, and make sure the settings are set to your local country and language. For most users this will be *United States* and *English*, respectively.

Click *Show Ideas and Statistics* for *Desktop and Laptop Devices*. This restricts searches to those done from desktop and laptop computers and does not include smartphones. While smartphones are a significant and growing source of traffic, smartphone traffic generally does not convert very well into revenue, and thus for the sake of conservatism we generally exclude this traffic from our analysis. For categories where mobile search is significant, run the search for *all mobile devices* and add these numbers to your *Desktop and Laptop Devices* to get the true volume.

> Enter site in *Website* box. Check *Only show closely related terms*. Set *Advanced Options*. Click *Search*.

Step 4: Enter Search Phrases

Enter the targeted keyword phrases in the *Word or Phrase* dialog box. Put each keyword phrase on a separate line. Double-check the search keywords to make sure there are no spelling mistakes. Click *Search* to perform the search and get your results.

> Enter keyword phrases in the *Word or Phrase* dialog box.

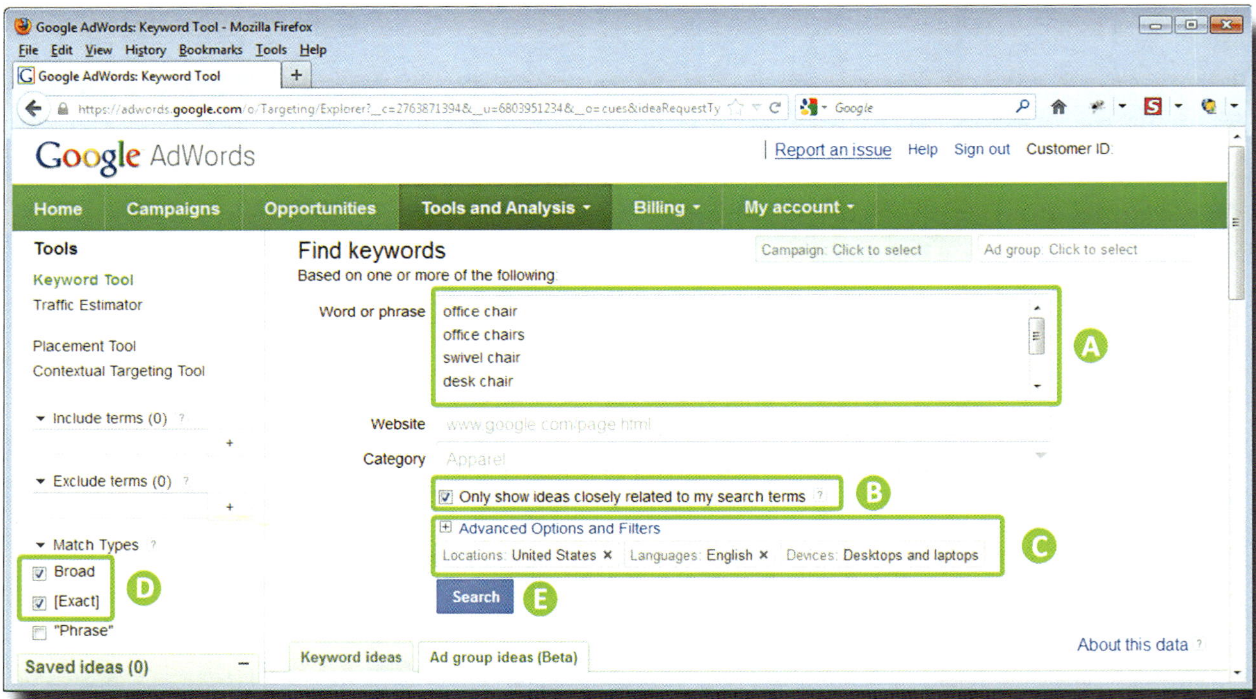

Figure 24 – (A) Enter keywords in the *Words or Phrase* dialog box.
(B) Click *Only show idea closely related to my search*.
(C) Set *Location* and *Language* and set devices to *Desktop and laptops*.
(D) Click *Match Type* checkboxes *Broad* and *[Exact]*.
(E) Click *Search*.

Step 5: Collect the Data

Select the *Keyword Ideas* tab when the results appear. The keywords entered will appear in the top window labeled *search terms*. To select these keywords, click the *Save all* button. (They can be cleared by going to the *Saved ideas* window on the bottom left of the screen and clicking the black cross that appears next to *My keyword ideas* when you hover your mouse over the words.) Download the keywords into a spreadsheet so that the data can be easily saved and manipulated. Click *Download* ⇨ *My keyword ideas* ⇨ *CSV for Excel*. Copy the data into the *Analysis* tab of your spreadsheet.

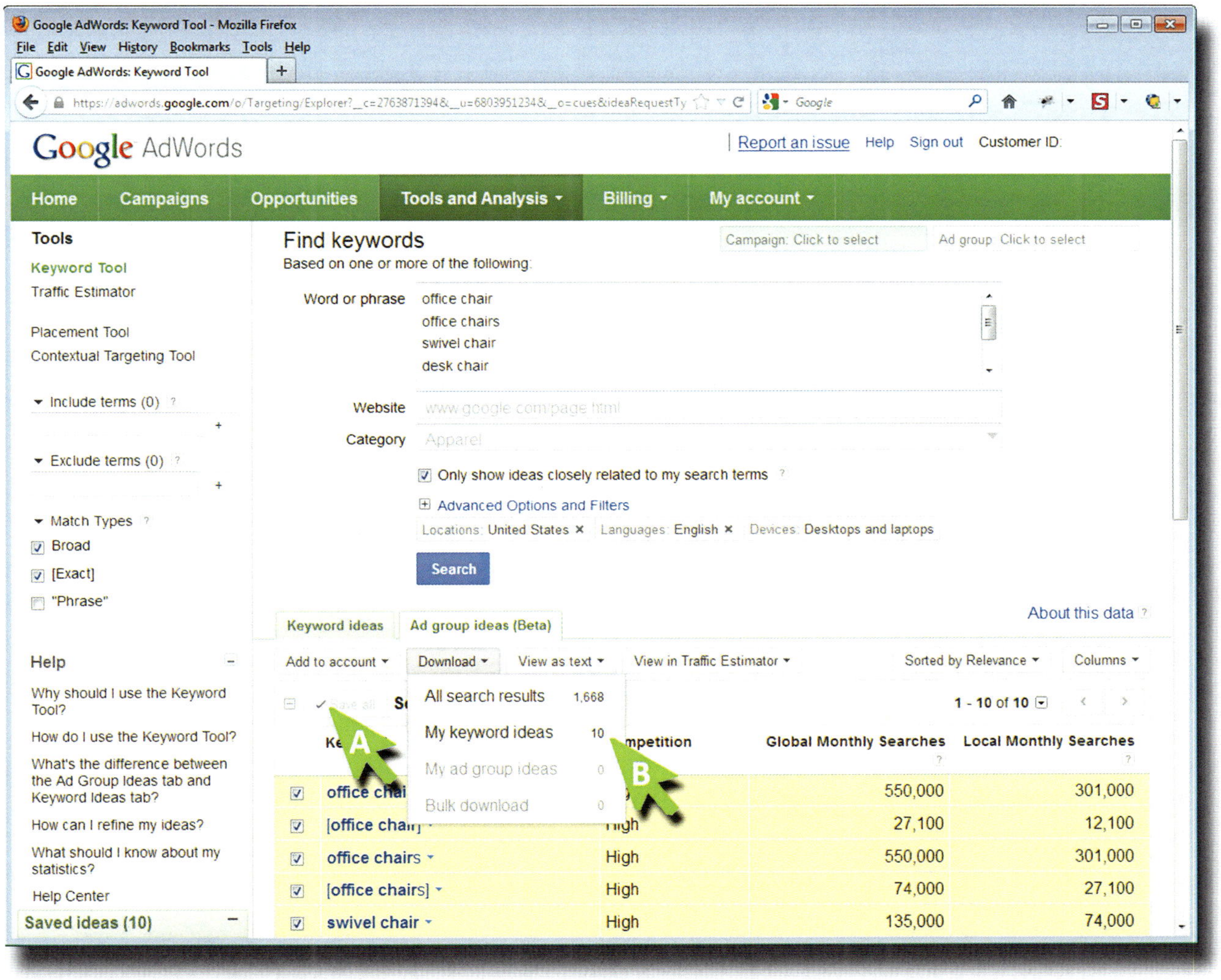

Figure 25 – (A) click *Save all* then (B) *Download* ⇨ *My keyword ideas*.

The data will contain three columns:

- **Competition** – A score from 0 (least competitive) to 1 (most competitive) indicating the amount of competition to purchase the keyword in the paid listings. However, this score does not tell you how difficult a keyword is to win using SEO. Consequently, we disregard this column.

- **Global Monthly Searches** – Displays the average number of monthly searches performed in the world (based on the prior 12 months).
- **Local Monthly Searches** – Displays the average number of monthly searches performed in the country that was selected in step 3 (based on the prior 12 months).

Only local data is useful for most businesses, because sales from overseas traffic are generally negligible. As such, most companies should record only local data. For international businesses, aggregate the numbers for local search from your main international markets (e.g., if your business is North American, sum Canada Local + Mexico Local + United States Local), or use the Global Monthly Search figure if your business is truly global.

You will note that each keyword appears twice on the list: once in [square brackets] representing exact matches, and once without the brackets representing broad matches.

Copy the relevant *Broad Search* and *Exact Search* data into the respective columns on the *Traffic Analysis* worksheet of the spreadsheet.

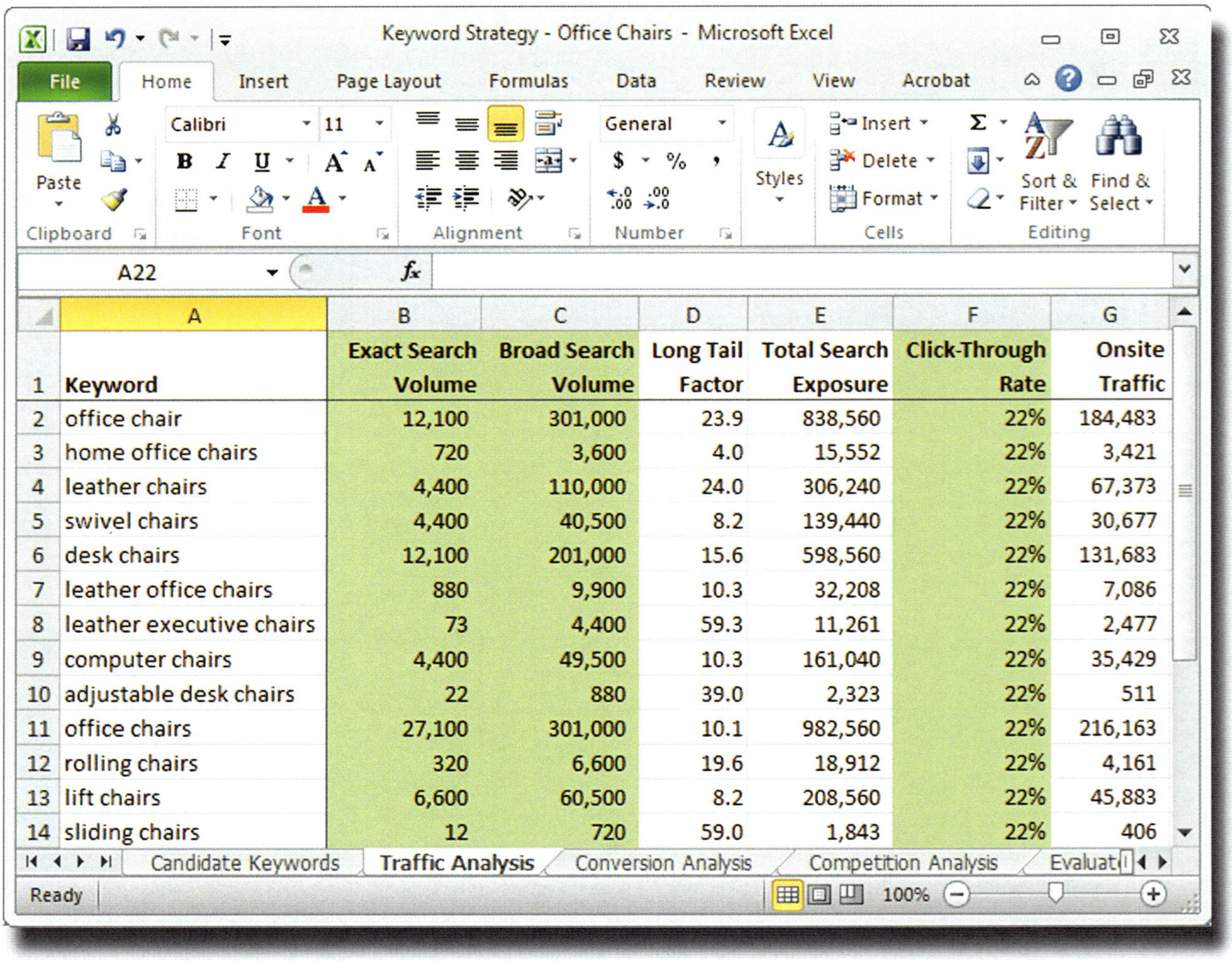

	A	B	C	D	E	F	G
1	Keyword	Exact Search Volume	Broad Search Volume	Long Tail Factor	Total Search Exposure	Click-Through Rate	Onsite Traffic
2	office chair	12,100	301,000	23.9	838,560	22%	184,483
3	home office chairs	720	3,600	4.0	15,552	22%	3,421
4	leather chairs	4,400	110,000	24.0	306,240	22%	67,373
5	swivel chairs	4,400	40,500	8.2	139,440	22%	30,677
6	desk chairs	12,100	201,000	15.6	598,560	22%	131,683
7	leather office chairs	880	9,900	10.3	32,208	22%	7,086
8	leather executive chairs	73	4,400	59.3	11,261	22%	2,477
9	computer chairs	4,400	49,500	10.3	161,040	22%	35,429
10	adjustable desk chairs	22	880	39.0	2,323	22%	511
11	office chairs	27,100	301,000	10.1	982,560	22%	216,163
12	rolling chairs	320	6,600	19.6	18,912	22%	4,161
13	lift chairs	6,600	60,500	8.2	208,560	22%	45,883
14	sliding chairs	12	720	59.0	1,843	22%	406

Figure 26 – Traffic data in Microsoft Excel.

Error Checking the Data

The numbers from Google Keyword Tools are occasionally wrong or misleading. If a number looks abnormal, particularly if it appears to be implausibly high, cross-check the number with another source. An easy way to validate Google numbers is to look at the data on Bing and Yahoo. Bing and Yahoo data is available in aggregate at http://www.bing.com/toolbox/webmaster/. Compare the Google:Bing ratios of keyword traffic for keywords where Google traffic data seems reasonable with the keywords where the data seems suspicious and correct the Google data accordingly.

Long Tail

Long tail keywords are keywords where the search volume is distributed among a large number of search terms, each with only a small amount of volume. Conversely, short tail keywords have search volume concentrated in a relatively few keywords.

For example, searches for *plumber* are massively fragmented (long tail). While there are over 2.2 million searches every month that contain the keyword *plumber*, only 27 thousand (0.1%) are for the exact word *plumber*. Those 2 million searches containing plumber are composed of hundreds of thousands of low volume searches like *Dallas plumber* (590), *Dallas TX plumber* (36) and *Dallas plumber reviews* (16).

In contrast, other keywords are more concentrated (short tail). For example, of the 60,000 broad searches associated with the word *unicycle*, 12,000 (20%) are for the exact word *unicycle*.

The length of the tail is a useful metric because it shows how much additional traffic is available if you optimize for keywords. If you win a long tailed keyword like *plumber* you are likely to pick up some of the long tail traffic with little or no extra effort.

Thus, all else being equal, keywords with long tail search volume are more attractive because you get more traffic from them than if the keyword did not have the accompanying long tail.

Calculate a Long Tail Factor for your keywords by dividing the non-exact match (i.e., broad-match searches less the exact-match searches) by the number of exact-match searches as follows:

$$\text{Long Tail Factor} = \frac{(\text{broad searches - exact searches})}{\text{exact searches}}$$

Using the unicycle example above, the Long Tail Factor is 4.

$$\text{Long Tail Factor} = \frac{(\text{Broad Searches - Exact Searches})}{\text{Exact Searches}}$$
$$= \frac{(60{,}000 \text{ searches/month - } 12{,}000 \text{ searches/month})}{12{,}000 \text{ searches/month}}$$
$$= 4$$

Again, a higher Long Tail Factor indicates searches for a keyword are spread out and include many variations. A low factor indicates that the search is concentrated in the exact keyword.

The Long Tail Factor is automatically calculated for each keyword in the *Long Tail Factor* column on the *Traffic Analysis* worksheet.

Search Exposure

To estimate the total amount of search traffic that a #1 position is likely to create, you need to account for the long tail as well as exact-match keyword traffic. The #1 position for a keyword phrase results in exposure to all the searches for that exact phrase. In addition, top ranked pages also tend to rank well for a significant portion of the associated long tail phrases with minimal extra effort.

Note: This only calculates the number of searchers that will see your search listing, not the fraction of searchers that will actually click-through to your site and become visitors. The click-through rate is covered in the following section of this chapter.

To calculate the total search traffic exposure, use the following formula:

$$\text{Total Search Exposure} = \text{Exact Searches} \times \left(1 + \frac{\text{Long Tail Factor}}{5}\right)$$

For example, returning to our unicycle example from the previous section, if we ranked #1 for *unicycle*, we would expect total search exposure to be 260,000 searches per year.

$$\text{Total Search Exposure} = \text{Exact Searches} \times \left(1 + \frac{\text{Long Tail Factor}}{5}\right)$$
$$= 12{,}000 \text{ searches/month} \times \left(1 + \frac{4}{5}\right) \times 12 \text{ months/yr}$$
$$\approx 260{,}000 \text{ searches per year}$$

Using the spreadsheet, the Total Search Exposure is automatically calculated

Click-Through Rate

The *Click-Through Rate* is the percentage of web searchers that will click on a listing and visit the site. Ranking #1 for a search term results in only some of the searchers visiting your site. While *organic yogurt* gets 880 searches per month, and the #1 site will be displayed at the top of the search listing for most of those 880 searches, not every searcher will click on the top listing. Some searchers click on lower ranked listings, some will click on the paid search listings, and some will not click on any result at all.

Estimate the predicted Click-Through Rate using the predicted Click-Through Rate for the search result position you are targeting. Below you will find average Click-Through Rates for the top ten organic search positions. Note, that there are many different ways of defining the Click-Through Rate and you will often see very different figures published by different sources. The figures we use take into account that some searchers will not click on any search results and some searchers will click on the paid search results. Thus, you will note that our Click-Through Rates to do not sum to 100%.

Position	Average Click-Through
1	22%
2	9.7%
3	5.7%
4	3.6%
5	3.1%
6	2.4%
7	1.7%
8	1.8%
9	1.3%
10	1.5%

Table 1 – Average Click-Through by Organic Search Position.

The figures in *Table 1* are averages. Expect deviations from these averages and adjust the projected click-through rates accordingly in the following circumstances:

- **Ambiguous Keywords** – Click-Through Rates for keywords that describe two or more things are lower than would otherwise be expected. This is often an issue with common high volume keywords. For example, a search for *cold* could be seeking a disease, a temperature, or even a band. Even within these categories there are ambiguities – a search for the cold (disease) could be seeking information about the disease, information about diagnosis, or information about treatment. Accordingly, you would expect lower than normal click-through rates in the top spot by a factor reflecting the distribution of searches. If you are promoting a cold remedy product and estimate only 30% of *cold* searches are relevant to your site, you would lower your Click-Through Rate (i.e., your predicted click-through rate for the #1 position would be 22% × 30% = 6.6%).

- **Branded Keywords** – Brand related keyword Click-Through Rates are higher in the first position and lower in subsequent positions. This is because most searchers are looking for the official website of the brand. The click-through for *Nordstrom* will be higher in the #1 spot (the official Nordstrom website) and lower in the subsequent positions. The click-through for the #1 position for a strong brand is typically around 85%, with the remainder of the search scattered throughout the other positions and non-clicks.

- **Informational Websites** – When authority informational sites like Wikipedia rank first in product-centric search results, the Click-Through Rate is higher in the second and subsequent ranked sites. For example, Wikipedia ranks #1 for the search *mortgage*, but since most searchers are after service providers they skip this first information-only listing resulting in higher click-through rates for the second and subsequent listings. Commercial websites second to Wikipedia for product-centric searches often enjoy Click-Through Rates comparable to top ranked sites. Conversely, for informational searches when authority informational sites (like Wikipedia) rank at #1 these sites exert a gravitational pull greater than a black hole, absorbing the vast majority of clicks. In these informational searches, commercial websites get a fraction of the clicks they would otherwise expect.

- **Google Rich Elements** – In the last few years Google began integrating extra elements into many search results. These extras provide information such as local providers, images, shipping results, related searches, and videos. These elements sometimes appear above the #1 organic listing. When elements display above organic results, the Click-Through Rate for the first regular organic search listings are reduced.

- **Shopping** – Searches that describe relevant products can result in Google Shopping results being displayed. Traffic in the top organic result is lowered by an average of 20% where these shopping results are above the first organic result.

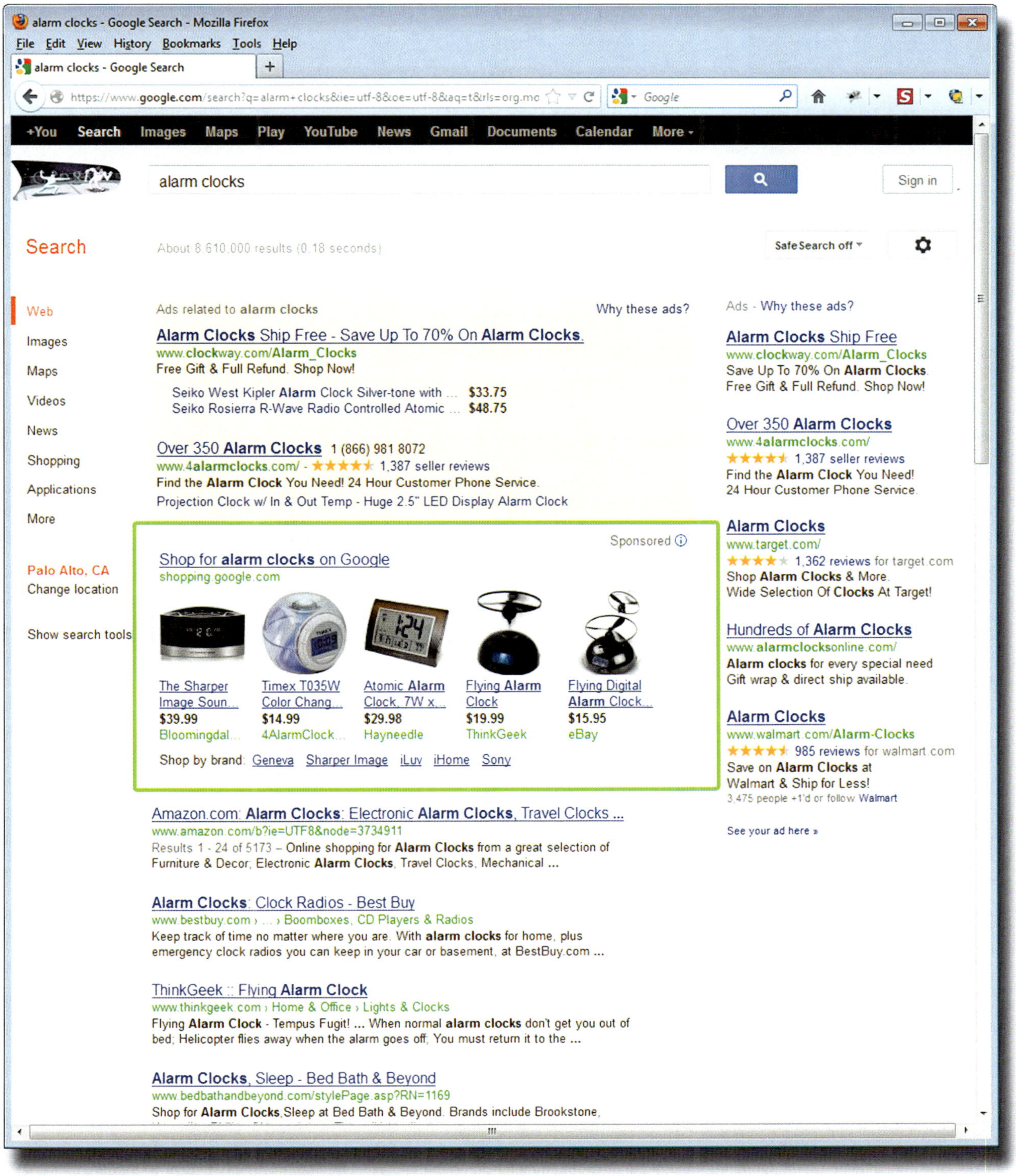

Figure 27 – Google Shopping Results.

- **Local** – Searches that are interpreted as related to a local business often result in a map and listings of local businesses. This forces the searcher to scroll down to find your listing, and accordingly, reduces click-through to about 60% less than what would otherwise be expected.

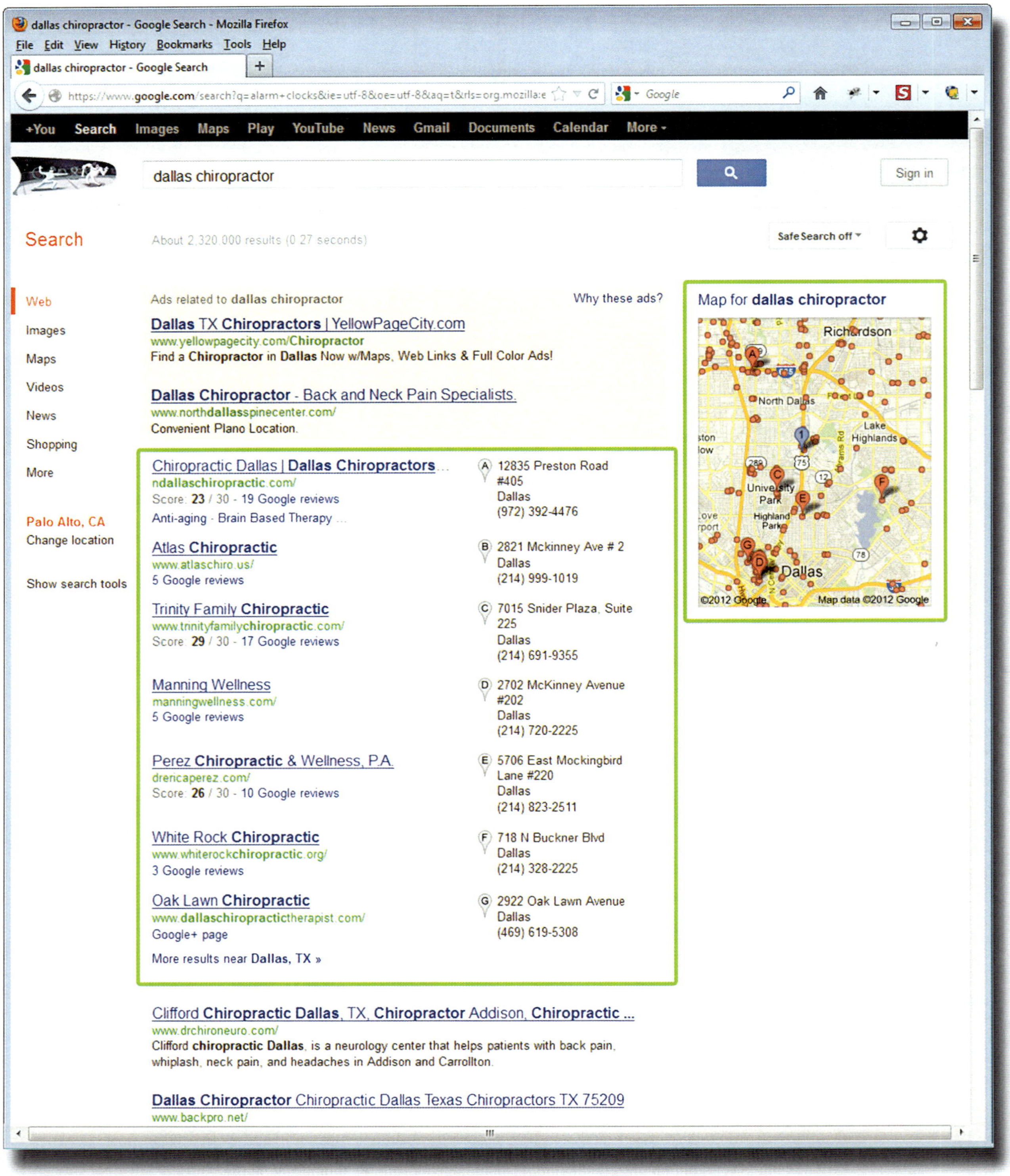

Figure 28 – Google Local Results.

- **Related** – If a search is vague or overly broad, Google will suggest related searches. These related search displays tend to reduce traffic by 15% below what would otherwise be expected.

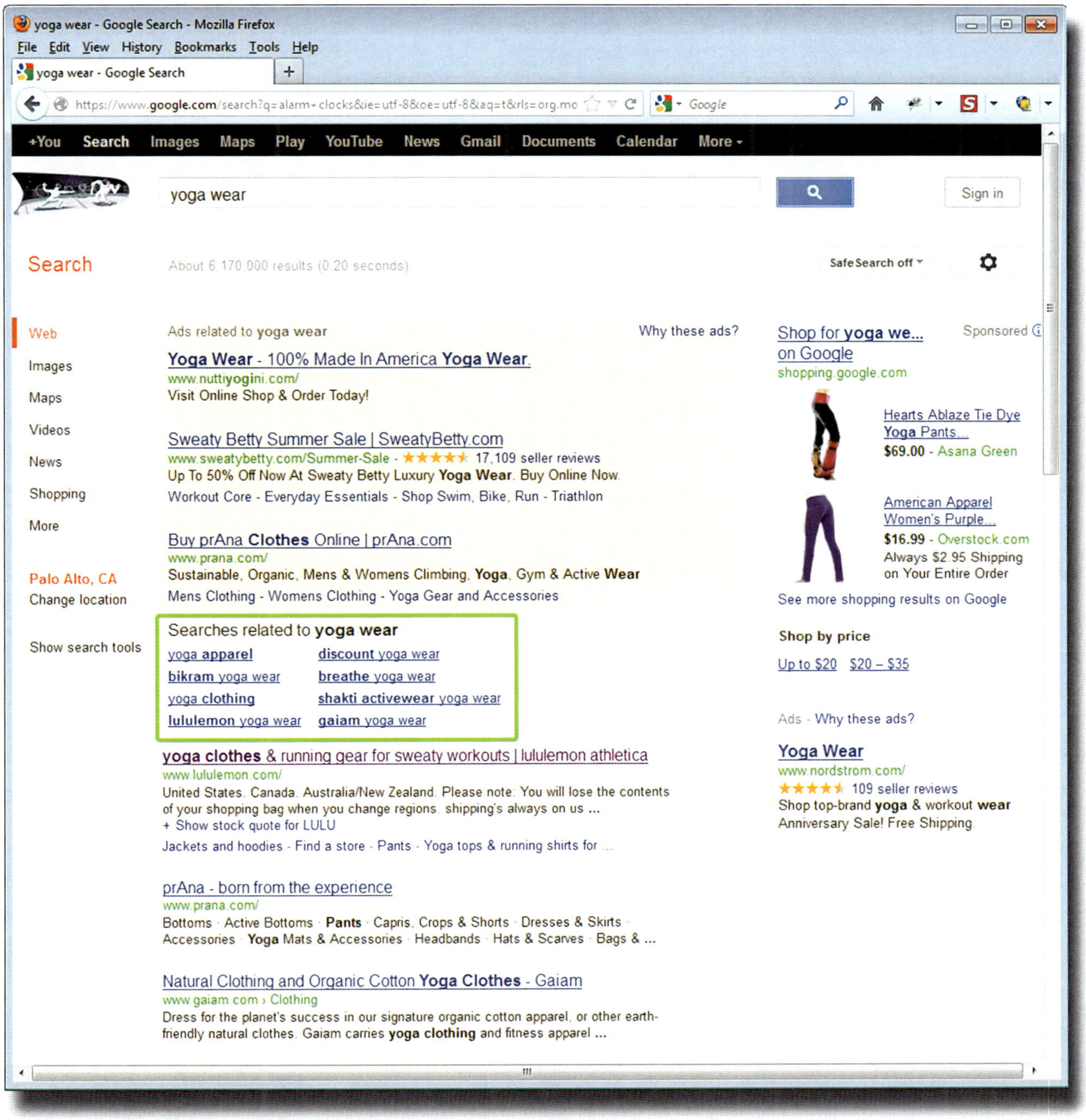

Figure 29 – Google Related Results.

Note, the display of Google Rich Elements above organic search results is not a death sentence. With sufficient SEO work your site can rank ahead of these Google Rich Elements and can even appear as the first listing in the Google Rich Element.

Pay-Per-Click Click-Through Rates

The best indicator of Click-Through Rate is the Click-Through Rate of the #1 position in Pay-Per-Click (PPC) advertising (the method for obtaining this data is described in the following chapter). If the Click-Through Rates for a #1 paid listing are less than 7% or greater than 12%, then the Click-Through Rate for the organic (non-paid) listing will likely be lower or higher than average. For the top position, every additional percentage point of click-through above or below this range usually translates into a two percentage point deviation in the click-through on an organic listing.

For example, if the PPC click-through rate for *silk slippers* was 15% for the #1 position in pay-per-click then the predicted organic Click-Through Rate would be as follows:

$$\begin{aligned}\text{Click-Through Rate} &= \text{Avg. SEO Click-Through Rate} + \left(\text{PPC Click-Through Rate} - 12\%\right) \times 2\\ &= 22\% + \left(15\% - 12\%\right) \times 2\\ &= 28\%\end{aligned}$$

If the PPC click-through rate for *silk slippers* was 5% for the #1 position in pay-per-click then the predicted organic Click-Through Rate would be as follows:

$$\begin{aligned}\text{Click-Through Rate} &= \text{Avg. SEO Click-Through Rate} + \left(\text{PPC Click-Through Rate} - 7\%\right) \times 2\\ &= 22\% + \left(5\% - 7\%\right) \times 2\\ &= 18\%\end{aligned}$$

Onsite Traffic

Use the Click-Through Rate in the following formula to translate the Search Traffic to Onsite Traffic:

$$\text{Onsite Traffic} = \text{Search Traffic} \times \text{Click-Through Rate}$$

The first position is the goal in most circumstance. However, when there is a very strong competitor in the top position, the second or third spot may be your initial objective. When targeting a lower position, estimate the amount of traffic using the lower click-through associated with that lower position.

For example, a #1 ranking for the keyword *unicycle* could be expected to yield 57,000 visitors per year.

$$\begin{aligned}\text{Onsite Traffic} &= \text{Search Traffic} \times \text{Click-Through Rate}\\ &= 260{,}000 \text{ searches/year} \times 22\% \text{ visits/search}\\ &\approx 57{,}000 \text{ visits per year}\end{aligned}$$

And a #3 ranking for the keyword *unicycle* could be expected to yield 25,000 visitors per year.

$$\begin{aligned}\text{Onsite Traffic} &= \text{Search Traffic} \times \text{Click-Through Rate}\\ &= 260{,}000 \text{ searches/year} \times 9.7\% \text{ visits/search}\\ &\approx 25{,}000 \text{ visits per year}\end{aligned}$$

Fill in the *Click-Through Rate* column on the *Traffic Analysis* worksheet. The *Onsite Traffic* will be automatically calculated for each keyword.

Traffic Trends

Trend data helps detect the existence of temporal patterns or irregularities in the search volume. For SEO purposes, the three types of trends that are interesting include macro trends that reflect ongoing changes in the market, seasonal trends that reflect changes in the market due to the time of year, and event based trends that reflect irregularities in the market.

Investigate trend data for all keywords where you think unusual traffic patterns are likely to be present. For the remaining keywords, just sample a few representative keywords to confirm your assumption that there are no unusual trends in the data. We examine trend data as follows:

Step 1: Navigate to Google Keyword Tool

Go to http://www.google.com/trends/.

> Go to google.com/trends/.

Step 2: Enter Keyword

Enter the keyword you are investigating into the search bar and click the *Search Trends* button.

> Enter keyword in search bar and click *Search Trends*.

Step 3: Set Your Region

Once results are displayed, change the regions drop-down box from *All regions* (which provides a global average), to your local region (United States for most of our readers). Note that keywords must meet a minimum threshold of traffic for trend data to be available. For smaller volume keywords assume the trends are the same as those found on similar higher volume keywords.

> Change *All Regions* drop down to target region.

Step 4: Interpret Data

The data is presented as an indexed time series graph that users can review to discern patterns or irregularities. You can adjust the time period of the data by using the drop-down box on the top right of the screen that reads, *All years*.

> Click *Export this page as a CSV file* ⇨ *CSV with relative scaling.* (optional)

To perform a quantitative analysis, download the data by clicking *Export this page as a CSV file* ⇨ *CSV with relative scaling*. However, in most cases, the patterns can be discerned from just the graph. We discuss some common patterns below. Record observations in the *Notes* column of the *Traffic Analysis* worksheet.

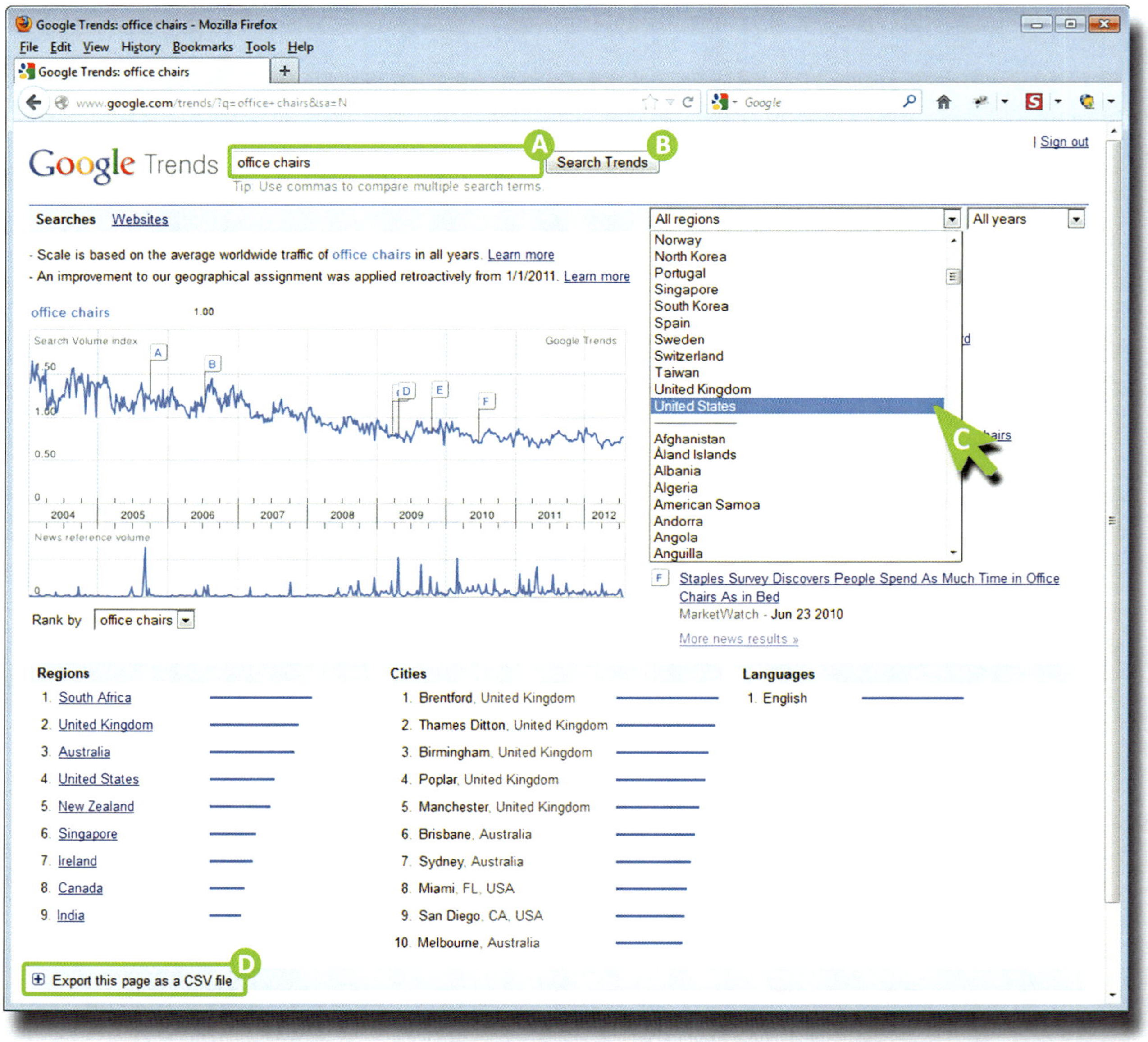

Figure 30 – (A) Enter keyword in search box. (B) Click *Search*.
(C) Select your *Region*.
(D) Click *Export this page as a CSV file* ⇨ *CSV with relative scaling.*

Macro Trends

Macro trends define whether the number of searches is increasing, decreasing, or holding steady over the years. For example, searches for *cordless phones* have been trending downward over the years as mobile phone use has grown. While there are 15,000 US searches each month for *cordless phones* reported by the Google Keyword Tool, the actual number of searches performed this month is likely lower since the number is based on a 12 month trailing average. And that number is likely to continue falling. So, expect there to be closer to 12,000 searches a month in one to two years, when your cordless phone SEO campaign is in full swing.

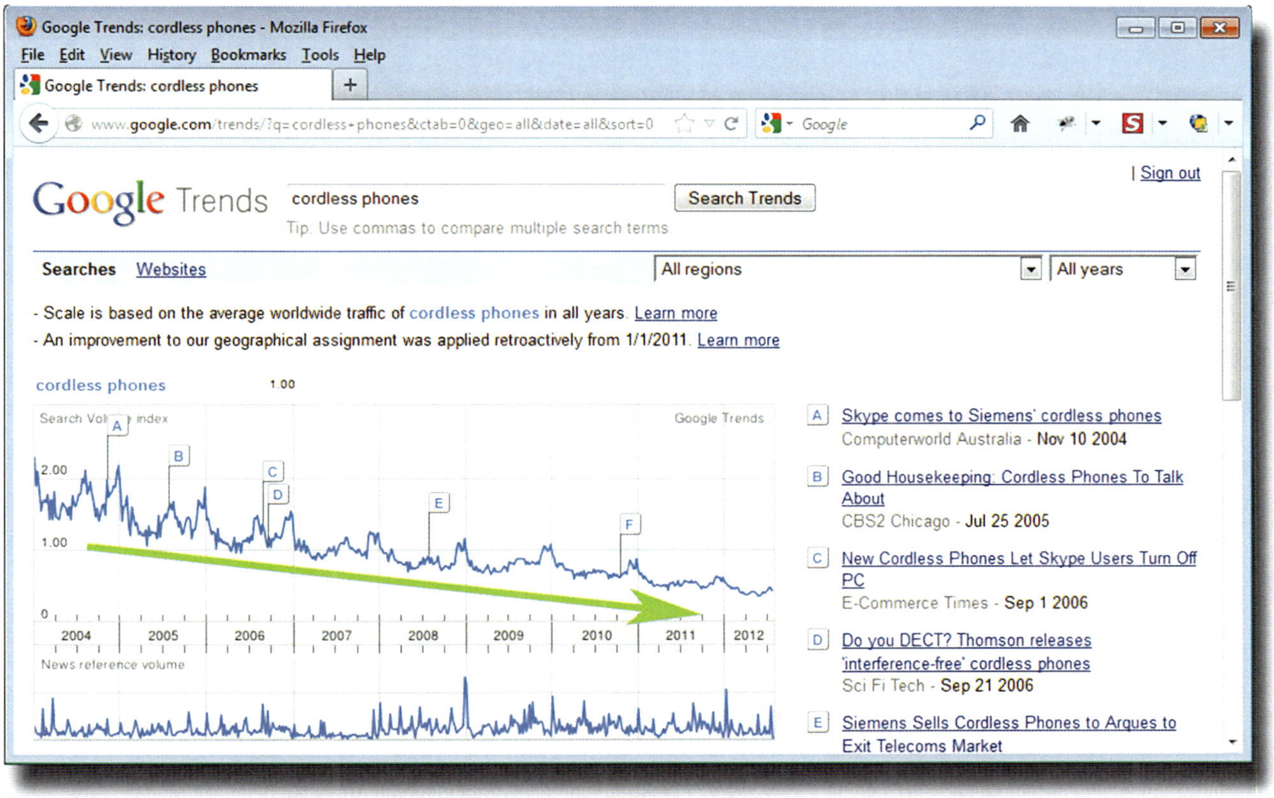

Figure 31 – Declining macro trend for *Cordless Phones.*

Conversely, searches for *3D printers* are increasing. The number of searches for *3D printers* is 60,000 per month based on a 12 month trailing average. This slightly understates the true number of searches that will occur this month, and vastly understates the number of searches that will likely be made in one to two years when your SEO labors start to bear real fruit.

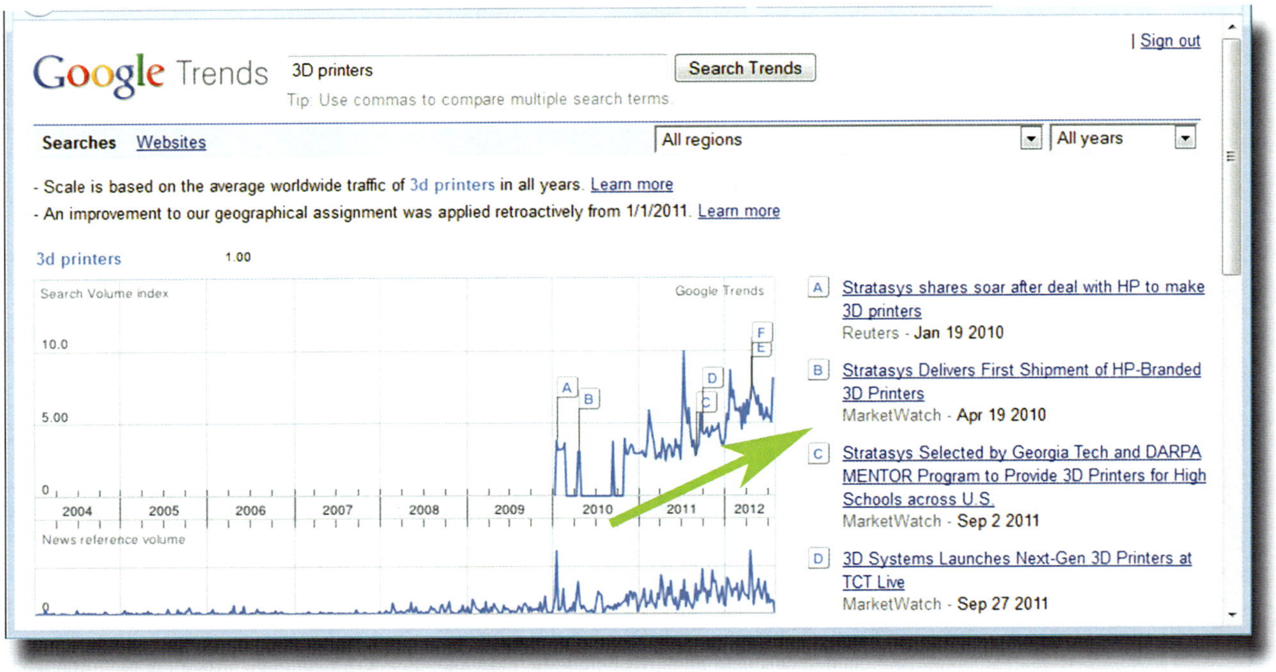

Figure 32 – Increasing macro trend for *3D Printers.*

Seasonal Trends

Search volume is often seasonal, meaning there are higher volumes at certain times of year. For example, searches for *Christmas trees* spike in November and December, but are virtually zero the rest of the year.

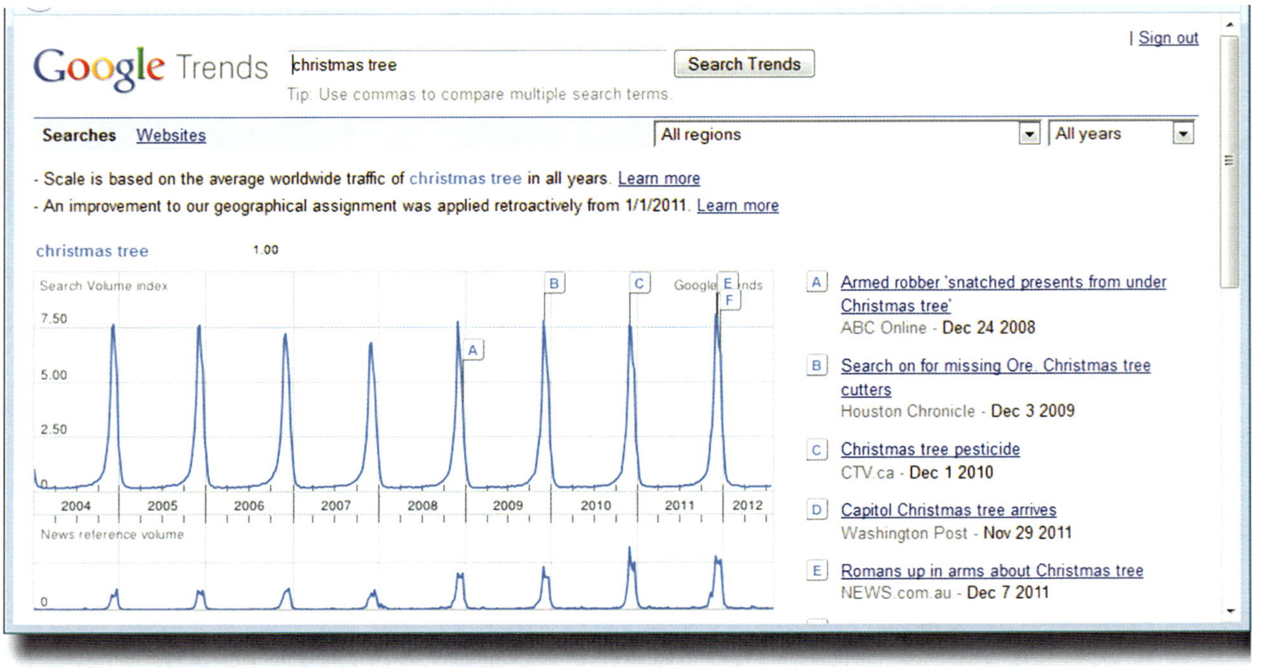

Figure 33 – Seasonal peaks in December for *Christmas tree* searches.

Understanding seasonality is important when planning an SEO campaign because seasonal peaks are the most important time to boast a high search rank. In the Christmas tree market, once you have established a solid baseline level of links, major SEO link building should only restart six months before Christmas while only a little maintenance is needed in the first six months of every year.

Event-Based Trends

Searches may also be triggered by news and events, resulting in misleading averages. For example, while the average number of searches for *Prince William* was 165,000 per month in 2011, most of those searches happened around the time of his wedding to Kate Middleton. Forecasting the likely number of future searches for this name based on the average would likely provide misleading numbers. An astute observer would review the trend data and predict the future average as being closer to 50,000 searches a month, with the occasional peak when events related to Prince William occur.

Figure 34 – Event-based peak for *Prince William* coinciding with his wedding.

Note any significant trend information in the *Notes* column of the *Traffic Analysis* worksheet.

Strategic Importance

Some keywords have special significance beyond volume. Mark keywords that have strategic significance, particularly if this significance is not reflected in the data.

For example, in working with startups commercializing a new technology, a new term will often have few searches. However, the startup knows the term is likely to become mainstream, at which time many companies will compete over it.

If you were a camera manufacturer, three years ago you might have had a strong hunch that *mirrorless camera* was going to be an important term in the future. As such, you would have optimized for the phrase to rank well for the term while it was less competitive. This strategy would have provided a platform for continued high ranking for the term in the future — when the term became more commercially significant.

Terms that have particular strategic importance should be noted in your evaluation and for these terms assessment should not be purely based on the numbers. Record these remarks in the *Notes* column of the *Traffic Analysis* worksheet.

Low Traffic Screen

After performing the traffic analysis, some terms will prove to have too little volume to be worth further consideration. Mark these low traffic keywords at this point to avoid any unnecessary analysis.

The threshold for excluding keywords will vary depending on the context of the conversion rate, profit margin, and the size of your enterprise. Small amounts of traffic are still worth targeting in industries where the conversion rate is good and the margins are high. In industries where the conversion rate is low and margins are low, the threshold for traffic is much higher.

For example, we have a client that provides highly specialized consulting services for banks. Their average contract generates around $200,000 worth of profit for the firm. They have few competitors, so leads convert efficiently into contracts — this is all to say their conversion is high. Even if a keyword generates an average of five searches a month, it still makes sense to optimize for this traffic because each site visitor represents such a high value.

On the other hand, we have a client that sells inexpensive clothing accessories with an average profit of $5 per order. The customers are largely window-shopping, so only 1-in-100 visitors becomes a customer. For that business it is not worth considering any keywords that generate less than 20,000 searches per year.

A good rule of thumb for a minimum monthly traffic threshold is as follows:

$$\text{Traffic Threshold} = \frac{\$1{,}000}{(\text{Conversion Rate} \times \text{Conversion Value})}$$

Thus if the average conversion rate for the keyword *silk slippers* was 1-in-100, and the average conversion value was $30, then the minimum threshold to make that primary keyword worth considering is 3,300 searches per year:

$$\begin{aligned}\text{Traffic Threshold} &= \frac{\$1{,}000}{(\text{Conversion Rate} \times \text{Conversion Value})} \\ &= \frac{\$1{,}000}{(1\% \times \$30)} \\ &= 3{,}300 \text{ searches per year}\end{aligned}$$

You will not have precise figures for these variables at this stage, so use conservative estimates. If your numbers were too conservative, you can always go back and rerun the analysis.

Trends and strategic significance also need to be taken into account when considering the minimum traffic threshold. Many startups are essentially inventing new categories. When getting started, there are very few searches for their technology, say *flying scooters*. But, they expect the number of searches to grow dramatically over time as they and their competitors get more publicity and grow the category. In these cases, use a three year projection for monthly search volume instead of the current volume.

Mark the keywords that do not meet the threshold and therefore need not be analyzed any further. Do this by highlighting the respective rows in red. Do not delete these keywords because you will use them later in the SEO process when undertaking on-page and off-page optimization.

Copy the remaining keywords into the *Keywords* column of the *Conversion Analysis* worksheet. Now that you know the volume of traffic, you need to understand what each of those searches is worth. For that information, we must analyze conversion.

4 Conversion Analysis

Summary: The goal of conversion analysis is to determine the value of each search to our enterprise. For each keyword assess the:

- **Conversion Rate** – The fraction of visitors to the site that make a purchase or take some other defined action.
- **Conversion Value** – The lifetime profit that a purchaser will generate for the business.

Using the conversion data, we can compute the value of winning each keyword.

"However beautiful the strategy, you should occasionally look at the results."
Winston Churchill, *Statesman* (1874 - 1965).

Conversion is a metric that depicts how effectively visitors translate to the aim of the website. The metric establishes the expectation for each visitor for a specific keyword and typically reflects how the visitor improves profit. The metric tells us the value of visitors to the enterprise and consequently informs decisions regarding the maximum level of investment to acquire these visitors.

For an e-commerce site that sells goods and services, conversion is measured using lifetime profit per unique visitor. Lifetime profit is simply the expected profit of a visitor during the entire tenure of that visitor's relationship with the business.

Combining the conversion metric with the traffic metric provides an approximation for how much the projected search traffic is worth, and consequently how much you should be willing to spend to win that keyword. For example, you might learn that winning *silk slippers* is worth $33,000 per year to your business, while *buy silk slippers* is only worth $1,000 per year.

For non-e-commerce sites, where direct sales are not the primary objective, the principle of conversion applies equally — even if not measured in terms of dollars of profit. Whether a website is an e-commerce site, a lead generation tool, or an issue advocacy site, it should

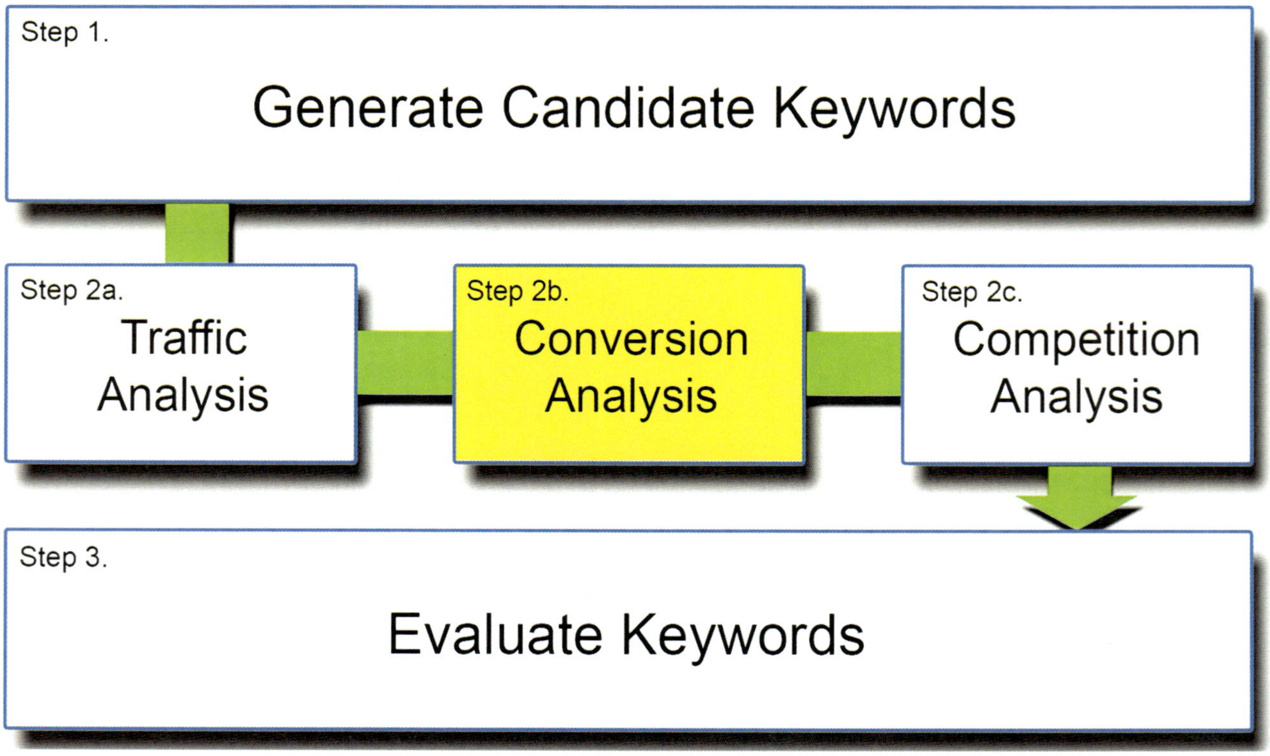

Figure 35 – Conversion analysis is step 2b of developing a keyword strategy.

have a goal and a way of measuring that goal.

For example, if a carpenter's site is intended to generate phone calls or emails from potential customers requesting a quote, an appropriate conversion metric could be customer contacts. While conversion for a site advocating a political candidate might be Facebook *likes* or registrations for an email list. Conversion for an informational site providing historical data about a town might be a visitor who spends more than three minutes browsing on the site or a visitor that navigates to three or more pages.

Thus while the conversion examples we use in this chapter are financial, you should not be so constrained. Conversion metrics should reflect the goal of the website.

Companies that rely on traffic data and ignore conversion run the risk of expending resources to acquire traffic that does not support their goals. The impact of this extends beyond the financial. An SEO campaign that generates a tremendous amount of traffic that does not convert can be greatly demoralizing to a company. The SEO team should be celebrating revenue growth instead of wondering why the traffic does not convert. These types of missteps may derail future SEO efforts as management or owners become unwilling to invest in further SEO efforts. On that cheery note, how do you predict conversion?

Look Before You Leap

An online seller of washing machines approached us to help improve their search position for *washing machine* and associated keywords. Washing machines are high cost items with low profit margins. However, we were excited about the opportunity due to the high level of traffic, and the high price point of the product. The client did not have any washing machine specific conversion rate data, but they knew that the rate of conversion for wall ovens was 1-in-300, and assumed a similar rate would apply to washing machines. We spent a lot of time and effort getting the client to #1 for washing machines. But, along the way, we noticed something odd. They were getting lots of traffic for *washing machines*, but only 1-in-1200 of these visitors turned into buyers.

A survey of site visitors found that most people searched with no intention of buying online. They were just doing research and would make the actual purchase at a local bricks-and-mortar store. For some unfathomable reason, customers were open to buying ovens online, but not washing machines. While people who research online and buy

continued

offline exist in every segment, in this segment the traffic was close to 100% offline buyers. Our client had only a regional bricks-and-mortar presence, so this traffic was not particularly valuable to them.

If we had spent a few thousand dollars testing we could have discovered this before spending a few hundred thousand dollars on SEO. Conversion is critical.

(Disguised client example)

When we talk about conversion, we are referring to the product of two components, *Conversion Rate* and *Conversion Value*:

- **Conversion Rate** – The rate at which visitors take the desired action, such as making a purchase (i.e., going from being visitors to customers).
- **Conversion Value** – The amount of profit the customer will generate over the course of their relationship with the site.

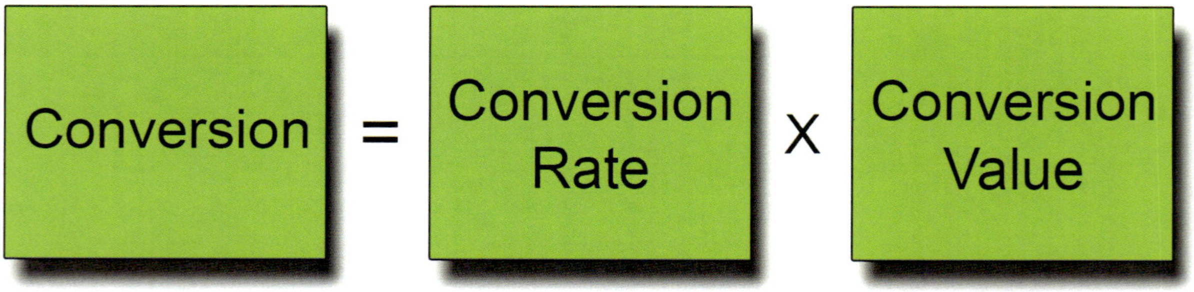

Figure 36 – Conversion = Conversion Rate x Conversion Value.

Conversion Rate

Once visitors get to your site, only a fraction of them buy something (or take whatever action you identified as your conversion objective). The *Conversion Rate* is defined as the fraction of visitors that take these desired actions. Conversion Rates vary considerably depending on the keyword a visitor uses, the industry, the product offering, pricing, and the quality of the website.

We primarily rely on data generated from Pay-Per-Click experiments to estimate the Conversion Rate for keyword traffic. Other methods such as using historical data and business judgment are cheaper and faster, but produce results that are markedly less reliable than using Pay-Per-Click testing.

Pay-Per-Click Conversion Rate Testing (PPC)

Purchasing Pay-Per-Click (PPC) advertising from Google is a quick way to acquire predictive conversion data. PPC advertising resembles the top organic listings and consequently provides good predictions for how SEO traffic will convert. Thus, we create our own paid listing and use this data to help us determine the Conversion Rate.

PPC advertising is displayed in Google above the natural (free / organic) search listings and to the right of the free search listings. These listings, particularly the listings that appear in the prime positions above the organic search results, are highly predictive of Click-Through Rates, Conversion Rates, and initial purchase values of the top position in the natural search results.

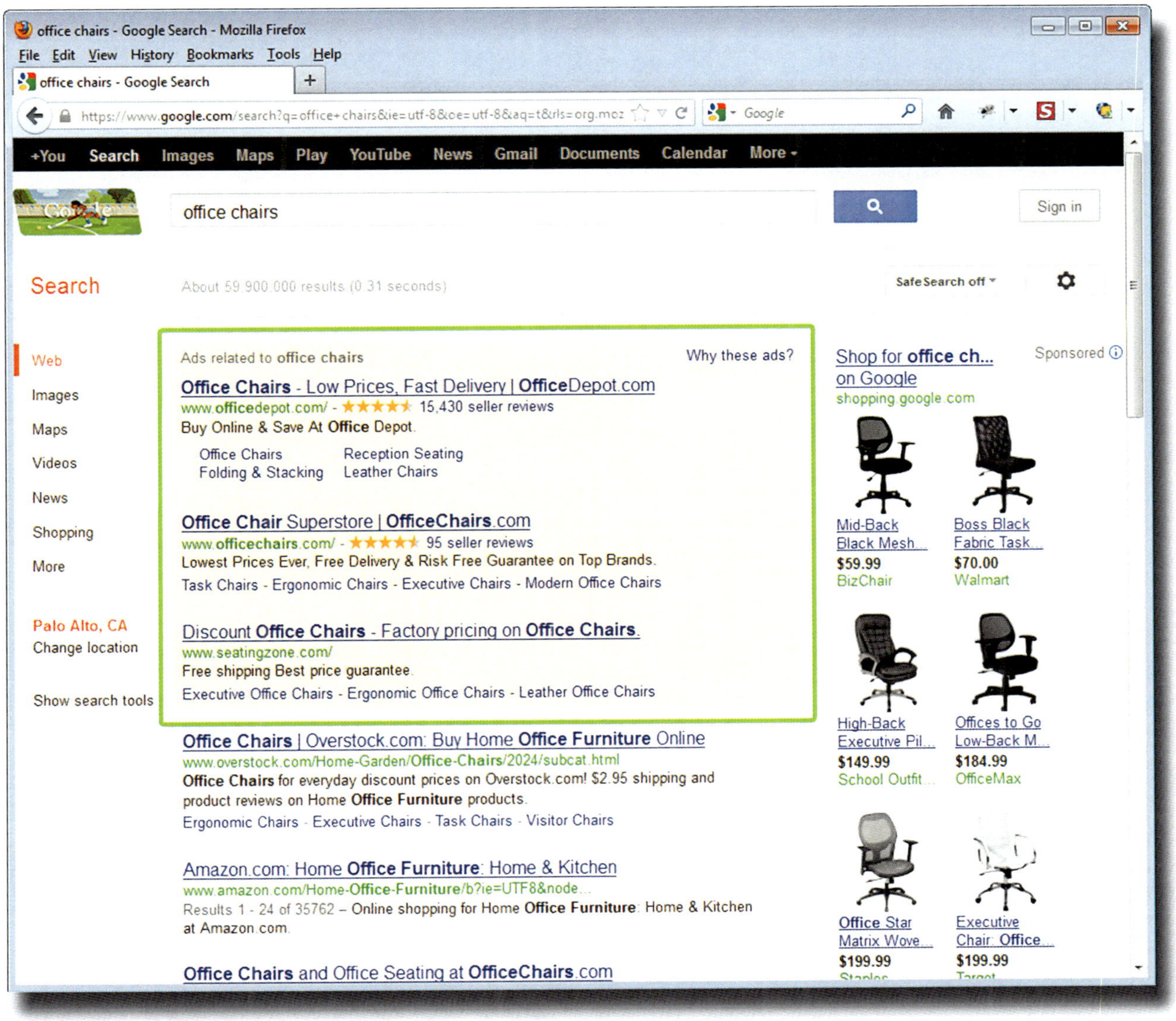

Figure 37 – The paid listings that appear above the organic listings provide data predicative of organic results.

The drawback of using PPC to test conversion is that you need to pay for the traffic. A typical set of tests will run from $2,000 to $10,000 depending on the number of keywords tested and the market price of the keywords. While a significant expense, PPC testing costs a small fraction of the expense of an SEO campaign. PPC trials can save hundreds of thousands of dollars in wasted SEO efforts to optimize for keywords that do not convert well.

A limitation of performing Pay-Per-Click testing is that there is usually not enough time to determine how many customers will become repeat purchasers. So, while you can generate an estimate of the likely initial purchase value of customers, you can't generate a lifetime value that is important in many types of businesses. For this reason, we usually supplement Pay-Per-Click data with historical data about the business.

To test the Conversion Rate using PPC traffic:

Step 1: Navigate to AdWords

Navigate to Google AdWords (http://adwords.google.com). You will need to have a Google AdWords account to log in.

Go to adwords.google.com.

Step 2: Link AdWords to Google Analytics

Be sure to link your Google AdWords account to your Google Analytics account so the two applications can exchange data. Google AdWords has rudimentary tracking capabilities, but Google Analytics offers a richer snapshot of the data. Install Google Analytics (http://www.google.com/analytics/) before proceeding, if you haven't already.

To do this:

(a) Go to *Tool & Analysis* ⇨ *Google Analytics*.

(b) Click *Admin*.

(c) Click the name of the Google Analytics account you are linking.

(d) Click *Data Sources*.

(e) Click *Link Accounts*.

(f) Select the *auto-tag by link* radio button on the popup and then select the relevant analytics profile from the dropdown menu. Click *Continue*.

For more details on linking Google AdWords and Google Analytics see: http://support.google.com/adwords/bin/answer.py?hl=en&answer=1704341

Step 3: Setup Conversion Tracking

Conversion tracking ensures that AdWords knows which customers made purchases and how much those purchases were worth. To setup conversion tracking you will need to add a bit of code to the purchase confirmation page so that when a customer makes a purchase, this information is tracked by AdWords.

Conversion tracking requires you to go into your website code. Ask your developer if uncomfortable going into the code yourself. It is a simple task and will take under an hour.

(a) On the top menu, select *Tools and Analysis ⇨ Conversions*.

(b) Click the *+ New Conversion* button.

(c) Enter a name such as *Store Purchase* then click *Save and Continue*.

(d) On the *Settings* page, enter the following:

(1) Conversion category: *Purchase / Sale.*

(2) Page security level: *HTTP* (if there is no SSL on your success page, this will be the most common setting); otherwise select *HTTPS*.

(3) Markup Language: *HTML* will be the most common. If in doubt ask your developer.

(4) Conversion Value: If all purchases have equal profit, enter it here. Otherwise, leave it blank and configure it directly in the code.

(5) Tracking indicator: *Don't add a notification to the code generated for my page*.

(6) Then click *Save and Continue*.

On the next screen you can choose to get the code or select the option to email the code to your developer. Whatever option you choose, you will get conversion tracking code that must be pasted into the body of the code for the purchase success screen (i.e., anywhere between the opening <body> and closing </body> tags).

Note: If your site sells multiple products, you will want to alter the code so that the amount of the profit per purchase variable is entered in place of the zero on the line:

var google_conversion_value = 0;

If your shopping cart cannot calculate profitability, then use the revenue figure. If revenue is used, don't forget to multiply it by your average profit margin before using it in the analysis.

For more details on configuring the profit per product, see: http://support.google.com/adwords/bin/answer.py?hl=en&answer=1722054.

Step 4: Payment

Enter billing information to pay for AdWords. Click the *Billing* tab and select *Preferences*, then follow the onscreen prompts to enter your credit card information.

Click *Billing* and then *Preferences*. Enter payment details.

There is an option to *prepay* or *postpay*. We suggest you *prepay* if you are new to AdWords because this limits the amount you spend. It is easy to accidentally spend a lot more than you intend on AdWords by misconfiguring a setting or leaving it active when you thought it was deactivated. Prepaying minimizes the impact of these potential mishaps.

Step 5: Create a New Campaign

Begin by creating a campaign that sets the default settings for all the individual keyword advertisements you will create later.

(a) Click the *Campaigns* tab.

Click *Campaigns* tab. Then *+ New campaign* ⇨ *Search Network only.*

(b) First time users click the big button on the left-hand side of the screen that says, *Create your first campaign*. Returning users click the *+ New campaign button* ⇨ *Search Network only.*

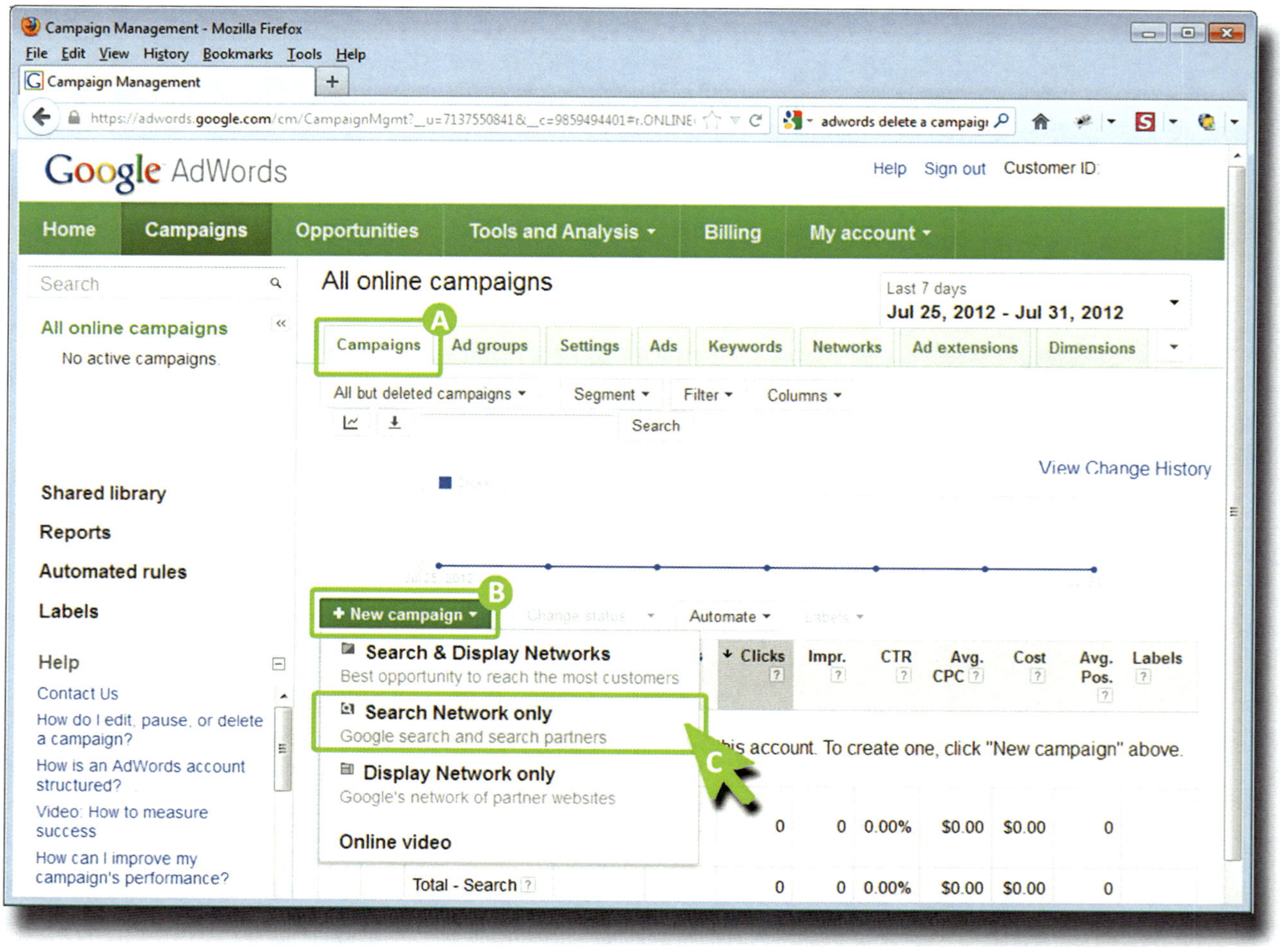

Figure 38 – Creating a new campaign in Google AdWords.
(A) Select *Campaign* tab.
(B) Click *+ New campaign* button.
(C) *Select Search Network* only.

Step 6: Configure Campaign

- **General** – Name the campaign to easily identify it in AdWords. A convention like *SITENAME Conversion Test DATE* works well. This name will not appear anywhere in the viewer search results.

- **Locations and Languages** – Enter the country and language you are targeting. For most users the options will be set to *United States* and *English*, respectively. If you are going to do multiple countries, set each as a separate campaign.

- **Networks** – Check the *Google search* check box. This ensures your advertisements are only displayed during Google Searches, and not on other sites. Google AdWords lets you advertise in all sorts of other places, like on third party websites, or YouTube videos; but we are not interested in those options while conducting this experiment.

- **Devices** – select *Let me choose...* then check only *Desktop and laptop computers*. This ensures that the PPC ads run only on Google search results on computers, excluding searches performed on smartphones and other mobile devices. This is preferable as mobile search generally does not convert as well and should be excluded from the experiment.

- **Bidding and budget** – Under the *Basic options*, select *I'll manually set my bids for clicks*. Then in *Default bid*, enter *0.01*. You will set the bids later when you configure individual keywords. In *Budget* enter *$200*. The *Budget* limits total spend to *$200* per day. This will be increased later when we are sure the campaign is working correctly. But, when getting started, keep the budget limits low to avoid making expensive mistakes. Under *Delivery Method*, select *standard*. This will spread the ads throughout the course of the day.

- **Save** – Click *Save and Continue*.

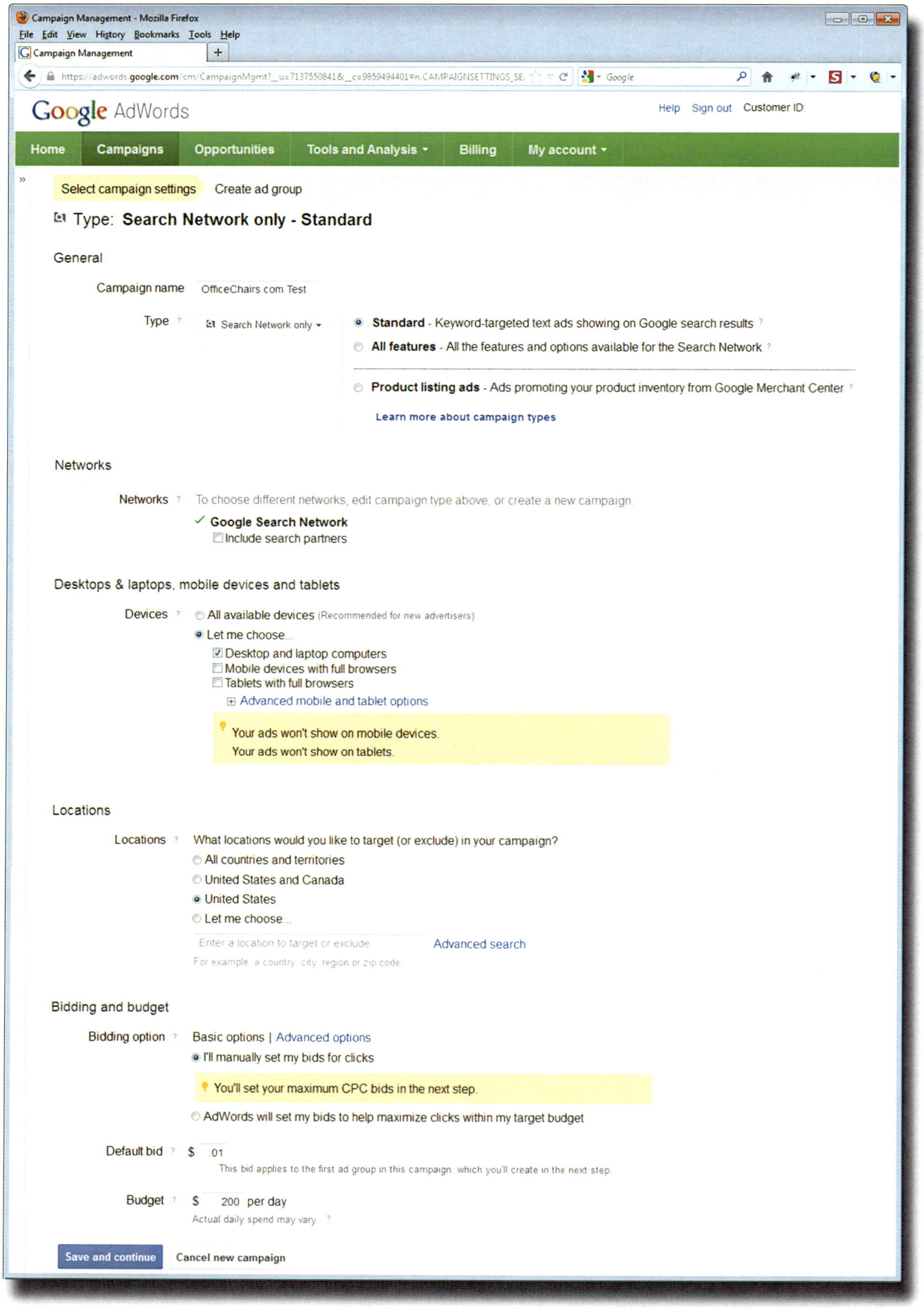

Figure 39 – Configuring your AdWords campaign.

Step 7: Create and Configure a new Ad Group

For each landing page that you are testing, create an *Ad Group*. *Ad Group* is Google's term to describe a set of keywords that trigger a particular advertisement and landing page. Keywords that all point to the same destination page and use the same advertising copy can share a single ad group. For example, testing three keywords for the homepage: *office chairs*, *desk chairs*, and *swivel chairs*, you could use the same Ad Group. While keywords that have different destination pages, or that require different advertising copy require their own Ad Groups.

The goal is to create an advertisement that is similar to what the webpage will display as an organic listing. So make the advertisement resemble, as closely as possible, an unpaid search engine listing.

(a) Click the *+ New ad group* button.

(b) Ad Group name – name the ad group after the landing page you are testing. For example, *Homepage*.

(c) Create an ad

  (1) Text Ad - Select the *Text ad* radio box.

  (2) Headline – Use the website title that appears when you search for the webpage.

  (3) Description line 1 and Description line 2 – Use the website description that appears when you search for the webpage.

  (4) Display URL – Use the true URL of the intended landing page. For example: www.homepage.com.

  (5) Destination URL – Again, use the true web address of the intended landing page. For example: www.homepage.com.

(d) Keywords – Enter the keywords you wish to test, placing each keyword on a new line and each keyword in square brackets (e.g., *[keyword1]*).

(e) Ad group bids – Enter your *maximum cost per click* default bid for the ad group. Set the bid at *0.01*. You will go back and individually enter a value for each keyword.

(f) Save – Click *Save and Continue*.

You will need to repeat this procedure for each ad group.

Figure 40 – Creating an Ad Group.

Step 8: Calculate Maximum Bid

> In menu select *Tools & Analysis ⇨ Traffic Estimator.* Enter a [keyword]. Click *Get estimates.* Find plateau point and add 10%.

AdWords works like an auction, assigning the top position to the site that bids the highest and has the highest click-through rate. You want your ad to appear in the top paid position because this most closely simulates the top organic position. To do this, you must be the highest bidder. You want to be a little aggressive in your bidding to make sure you win, but you also don't want to significantly overpay.

Navigate to the AdWords Traffic Estimator by selecting *Tools & Analysis ⇨ Traffic Estimator.*

Enter one of the keywords in square brackets (e.g., *[keyword1]*) and click the *Get estimates* button. A chart with results will appear. At the top of the chart will be a *Locations* and *Language* menu that you can change to suit your target audience (for most of our readers this will be *United States* and *English*, respectively). The adjacent *Networks* menu should be set to *Google Search.*

Note the plateau point on the chart where the line starts to flatten. This is the point where increasing your bid does not add considerably to the number of clicks. Take this plateau price and add 10%. Repeat this step for each keyword you are testing.

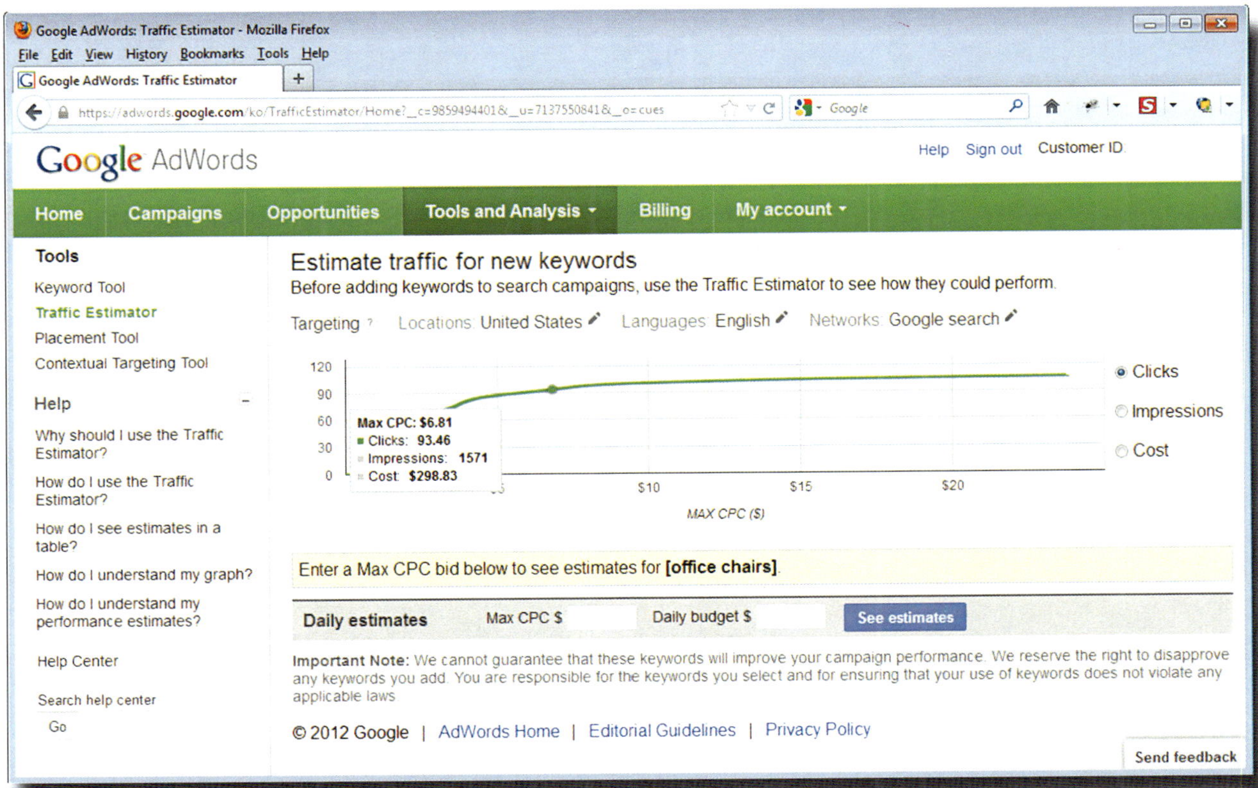

Figure 41 – Find the plateau point on the Keyword Estimator Graph and add 10% to find your starting bid.

Step 9: Set Maximum Bids

Now set the bids for each of your keywords using the winning bid estimates you generated in the previous step.

(a) Click the *Campaigns* tab, then select your campaign from the left hand list of campaigns.

(b) Click the *Keywords* tab.

(c) Check all the keywords by clicking the check box at the top.

(d) Select *Edit* (a popup will appear), click yes to clear it.

(e) Enter the relevant bid for each keyword from the previous step.

(f) Click *Save*.

(g) If you are not getting traffic, or your listing is not appearing as #1, return to this screen and increase your maximum bid.

It may take a couple of days for your advertisements to display. This is because Google manually reviews some advertisements; particularly those associated with new accounts. But, within three days advertisements should appear at the top of the Google results for the keyword phrases you selected.

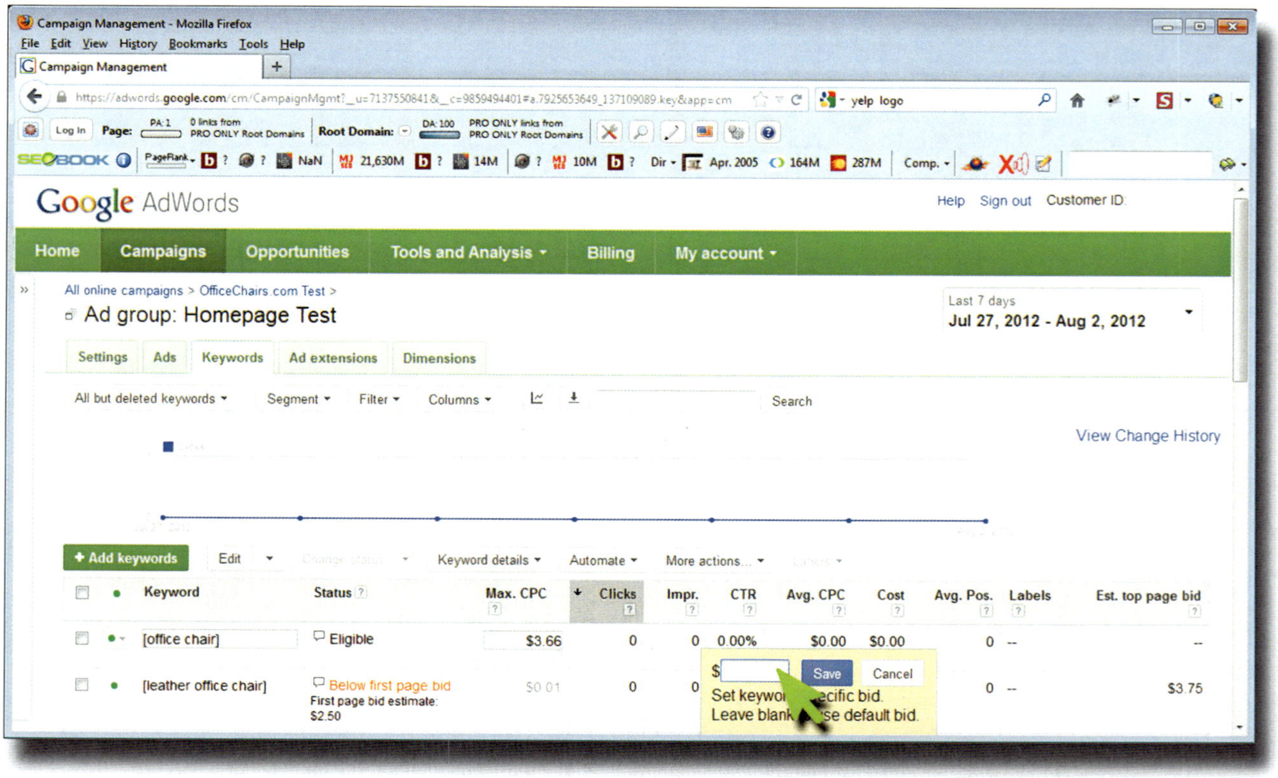

Figure 42 – Set AdWords bids.

Step 10: Monitor

Finally, monitor the results of the keyword tests to help inform your keyword strategy decisions.

(a) Click the *Campaign* tab and select your campaign. Then click the lower *Keywords* tab to see the results broken down for each keyword.

(b) Set the date range in the top right-hand corner to include the relevant days. The data usually lags four hours, but can take up to a day to display. This means you may not be viewing all the data for the activity in the last twenty-four hours. Also note that conversion in some niches lags several days (i.e., a viewer comes to the site but only decides to buy a few days later). Google AdWords captures conversions up to thirty days later. If you know your customers are slow to buy, wait thirty days after you have finished running your experiment to fully evaluate the data. However, in most industry segments waiting just two or three days is sufficient.

(c) Check the *Avg. Pos.* (Average Position) column for all keywords. This shows the average position the advertisement appears. You want the number to be close to one because this best simulates the top organic position in Google. Issues with average position happen when few people are selecting your advertisement or your bid is too low. If the position is greater than 1.4, increase your bid (see previous step).

(d) Check the *CTR* (Click-through Rate) column for all keywords. This shows the percentage of time the ad was displayed and the number of times someone clicked on the advertisement.

(e) Check the *Conv. Rate* column (Conversion Rate). This is the number of times that someone clicked the ad and bought something.

(f) Check the number of clicks. The statistics above are only reliable if you have a sufficiently large sample.

(g) Download the data for further analysis by clicking the download icon.

Take the Conversion Rate that you have calculated for each keyword and add it to the *Conversion Rate* column in the *Conversion Analysis* tab of the spreadsheet.

Step 11: Deactivating the Campaign

As you accumulate adequate data for each keyword, switch off the keyword advertisements to avoid spending money acquiring unneeded additional data.

(a) Click the *Campaign* Tab, select your campaign, and click the lower *Keywords tab* to see the results broken down for each keyword.

Sample Size

Q: How many clicks do I need to purchase for each keyword?

A: More clicks result in more reliable predictions of the value of traffic. However, there is a monetary and time expense associated with acquiring this data. A good rule of thumb is that you need enough clicks to get ten conversions. The number of clicks is thus equal to ten divided by the Conversion Rate (with a minimum of 100 clicks).

$$\text{Sample Size} = \frac{10}{\text{Conversion Rate}}$$

For example if your Conversion Rate is equal to 3% (1-in-33), then you will need to purchase around 300 clicks (10/0.03).

(b) To turn off an individual keyword, click the green circle next to the keyword, and select the *Paused* option.

(c) Once you have completely finished with the campaign, switch the entire campaign off to be certain the campaign is deactivated. Click the *Campaign* Tab. Click the green dot next to the campaign you want to deactivate and select the *Paused* option.

Testing Clusters

To reduce cost, combine lower value keywords and keywords that are likely to be very similar in terms of value. For example, if you were interested in the keywords *silk slippers*, *slippers silk*, and *slippers made of silk*, you could make the assumption that the value of these keywords is similar.

A word of caution: When making these assumptions, small differences in the search terms can create large differences in the Conversion Values that defy any logical explanation. Avoid making these assumptions for keywords where you plan to make large investments.

For example, a client observed the following discrepancy in Conversion Rates for the following two phrases that common sense would suggest should be identical:

- Dogs water bowl (1.2%)
- Water bowl for dogs (2.5%)

Typical Conversion Rates

If you cannot or will not test conversion rates, you can use the average conversion rates provided in the table below. But a word of caution cowboy, these rates are averages based on small samples of US websites. There can be wide divergences from these number in both directions and we would strongly advise against their use when you have the ability to perform conversion testing experiments that will yield more reliable results.

Adjust the conversion rates according to market factors. Adjust rates downward where there is a lot of competition, where your site is less price competitive and where your market is a commodity market. Adjust conversion rates upward where there is limited competition, where you are a price leader, where your product is highly differentiated, where the purchase is time sensitive, or where you are in a B2B market.

Site Type	Avg. Conversion Rate
E-commerce (0 - $30)	3.0 %
E-commerce ($30 - $100)	1.5 %
E-commerce ($100 - $300)	1.0 %
E-commerce ($300 - $1,000)	0.7 %
E-commerce ($1,000 +)	0.5 %
Online Services (free)	10.0 %
Online Services (paid)	1.0 %
Local Services (plumber, physician, etc)	3.0 %
Adsense	5.0 %

Table 2 – Average Conversion Rates by website type.

Now that we know what fraction of visitors will turn into customers, we need to investigate what each of those customers is worth to the business.

Conversion Value

A customer's value often extends beyond their initial transaction. A new customer can result in multiple transactions over time. A customer may also be a source of referrals that lead to additional purchases from friends and family. Therefore, the aggregate value of all these transactions must be calculated to properly affix a value to the customer and their patronage.

One-Off Purchases

The lifetime revenue from a one-and-done customer is going to be equal to the revenue from the initial transaction.

For example, if you sell only kitchen scales, a customer who buys a pair of scales is unlikely to buy another item. The occasional customer might buy a second pair for a friend or to replace a broken pair. But generally the initial transaction is the only transaction with each customer. In these cases, assume that the only purchase is the initial purchase when you model the value of a customer.

To determine the value of purchases, determine what your keyword customers are purchasing and the margin on these products. For this you can use the PPC experimental data generated in the step above (as captured by Google Analytics).

(a) Log into Google Analytics (http://www.google.com/analytics/) and select the relevant site.

(b) Go to *Conversion* ⇨ *Product Performance*.

(c) Select only the Pay-Per-Click Visitors by clicking *Advanced Segments*, then clicking the radio box *Paid Search Traffic* and deselecting any other check box. Then click the *Apply* button.

(d) Select the appropriate date range by clicking the date in the top right corner of the page and selecting the starting date and ending date.

(e) Click *Secondary Dimension*, then *Advertising*, then *Keyword* to get a list of the search keywords that produced the purchase.

(f) A list and quantity of products purchased, is displayed. Download this data by clicking the *Export button*, then *TSV for Excel*, then *Save the file*.

(g) Add a marginal profit column within the Excel file for each product that generates significant profit. Calculate the marginal profit for each unit sold. This is the revenue less the cost of goods sold. Include an allowance for projected returns and customer service. DO NOT include fixed costs in your calculation (i.e., the cost of your warehouse).

(h) Multiply the marginal profit by the number of purchases for each keyword. This should produce the total profit from your campaign for each keyword. Divide this by the number of unique purchasers for each keyword to get the average profit per keyword.

Recurrent Purchasers

Some enterprises are more conducive to repeat transactions. This is particularly the case where your product involves an ongoing subscription model, has consumables, or leads to complementary purchases.

For example, if instead of only kitchen scales, you sold high-end kitchen equipment, a significant fraction of the customers that bought scales could be expected to return and make other purchases such as a mixer or a knife set.

For a website with a significant amount of repeat business, the lifetime value of the customer needs to be used rather than just the initial purchase profit. The initial purchase profit, as calculated above, will underestimate the worth of search traffic, and consequently cause you to miss profitable opportunities to expand the business.

Historic data is often a good source for determining the lifetime value of a customer. While Pay-Per-Click experiments allow you to estimate the initial value of the customer, since these experiments will be relatively new, you don't get an accurate idea of how much the newly acquired customer will spend over their lifetime.

It often takes many years to realize the full value of the customer, thus using an experimental methodology like purchasing Pay-Per-Click traffic will take too long to bear dependable results. Utilize historical data instead.

If your business is new and historical data is unavailable, attempt to obtain data from a friendly competitor in the same industry or extrapolate from similar businesses where you do have access to data. At a minimum, project the likely lifetime value of the customer by extrapolating from the longitudinal customer data you do have from your own business.

Some e-commerce platforms show repeat purchase data which makes internal analysis easy. If your platform lacks this functionality, export all previous purchases and match purchases made by the same person or the same address. Use this to approximate a repeat purchase rate, and the likely additional margin contributed by these repeat purchases.

Startups Without Revenue

Many early stage companies do not have a mechanism for monetization. These enterprises assume that building a large network of engaged users can be monetized, typically through targeted advertising. Initially, monetization takes a back seat to growth and scale. For these businesses, a value per user must still be assigned to new users to guide investments in user acquisition.

Estimate the value per new user based on benchmarks from companies that have gone public, been acquired, or taken a recent round of funding.

Determine where your business fits in along this spectrum. In the best case, a site attracts high frequency users and highly commercializable traffic. For example, an average Google user visits the site multiple times per day and a sizable fraction of the visits involve searches related to commercial products that are attractive to advertisers. Thus, a Google user is worth nearly $200.

On the other end of the spectrum are users where the level of engagement is lower, and where the traffic has less commercial value. For example, an average Yelp user visits the site only a few times a month. The Yelp user is also less receptive to advertising, as they are only looking for impartial consumer reviews. Consequently, Yelp users are worth closer to $20 per user.

The amount you should invest in new users is also a function of maturity. For most startups there are significant network effects to the service. And early users evangelize the service to their network, in-turn attracting new users. Thus the value of early users have a multiplier attached to them. As the business matures and growth plateaus, the late adopters have no attached multiplier on their value, because they do not tend to attract many other users, nor add significantly to the network effect.

For example, if you were starting a new *Instagram*, you might be willing to spend $100 per user to attract your first 10,000 users – because those first users will seed widespread adoption. But, as the business matures and your brand becomes ubiquitous, new users are worth less because they contribute little to further adoption and are worth only whatever revenue can be attributed to an incremental user. After you acquire 100 million users, you might now only be willing to pay $10 to acquire each new user.

Also factor in capital constraints. If capital is a limiting factor in your decision making, consider alternatives for user acquisition. If there are alternative methods for acquiring users, such as PPC advertising or public relations, the per-user acquisition costs for these other methods will form a ceiling on the price you are willing to pay to acquire new users.

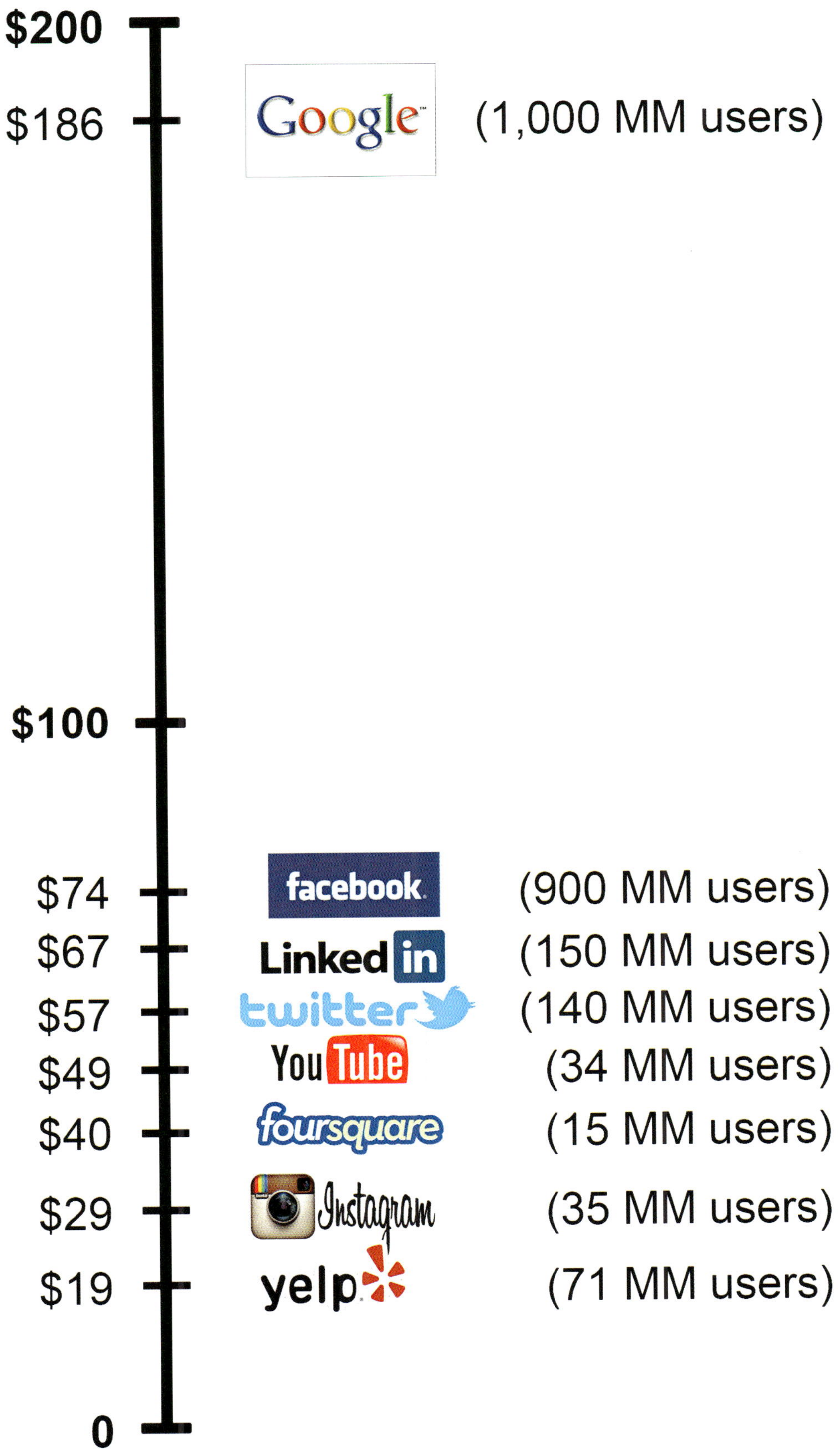

Figure 43 – Value per user benchmarks for advertising supported businesses.
(July 2012)

Once you have determined the Conversion Value for each keyword, enter it in the *Conversion Rate* column in the *Conversion Analysis* worksheet.

Calculating Conversion Factor

The *Conversion Factor* is calculated by multiplying the *Conversion Rate* by the *Conversion Value*. This tells you how much a visitor from a keyword is worth.

> Conversion Factor = Conversion Rate x Conversion Value

For example, if the Conversion Rate is 2%, and the lifetime value of the customer is $55 for the keyword *silk slippers*, then the Conversion Factor is $1.10 as calculated below:

Conversion Factor = Conversion Rate x Conversion Value

= 0.02 customers/visitor x $55 /customer

= $1.10 per visitor

This means the average visitor for the keyword *silk slippers* is worth $1.10 of profit to your business. This Conversion Factor gives you a way to quantify the value of the visitors produced by a keyword.

The Conversion Factor is automatically calculated in the *Conversion Factor* column of the *Conversion Analysis* worksheet.

If some of the keywords have anomalously low Conversion Factors and lack any other redeeming qualities, mark them to be removed from further analysis. Take the remaining keywords and copy them to the *Keywords* column of the *Competition Analysis* worksheet and the *Evaluate Keywords* worksheet.

Now that you know the volume and value of search traffic for each keyword, it is time to determine how much work it will take to get your website to outrank the competition.

5 Competition Analysis

Summary: Determining the amount of work required to rank in the #1 position for a keyword depends on the amount of SEO competition. To quantify the level of competition for each keyword, use the following data points:

- **Number of Links** – The number of inbound links from unique websites.

- **Page Authority** – The overall authority awarded to a site by virtue of having links from other trustworthy sites.

- **Anchor Text** – The fraction of links pointing to a site that contain the anchor text relevant to the targeted keyword.

Compare your scores in these metrics to those of your competitors and estimate the cost to outrank your competitors.

"Every morning in Africa, a gazelle wakes up. It knows it must outrun the fastest lion or it will be killed. Every morning in Africa, a lion wakes up. It knows it must run faster than the slowest gazelle, or it will starve. It doesn't matter whether you're a lion or a gazelle--when the sun comes up, you'd better be running."

Roger Bannister, *Athlete* (1929 -)

When evaluating opportunities, benchmark the competition against your site to understand how much ground you need to cover to compete. This benchmarking information lets you estimate the cost required to win the coveted #1 spot. This, in turn, enables you to make the determination of whether the reward for getting to #1 justifies the SEO cost.

There are many factors that determine search rank (these factors are covered in-depth in our books on SEO on-page and SEO off-page optimization), but the number and quality of inbound links is the dominant and most expensive factor. Therefore, the critical comparison is — the number and quality of your competitors' inbound links as compared to the number and quality of your own inbound links.

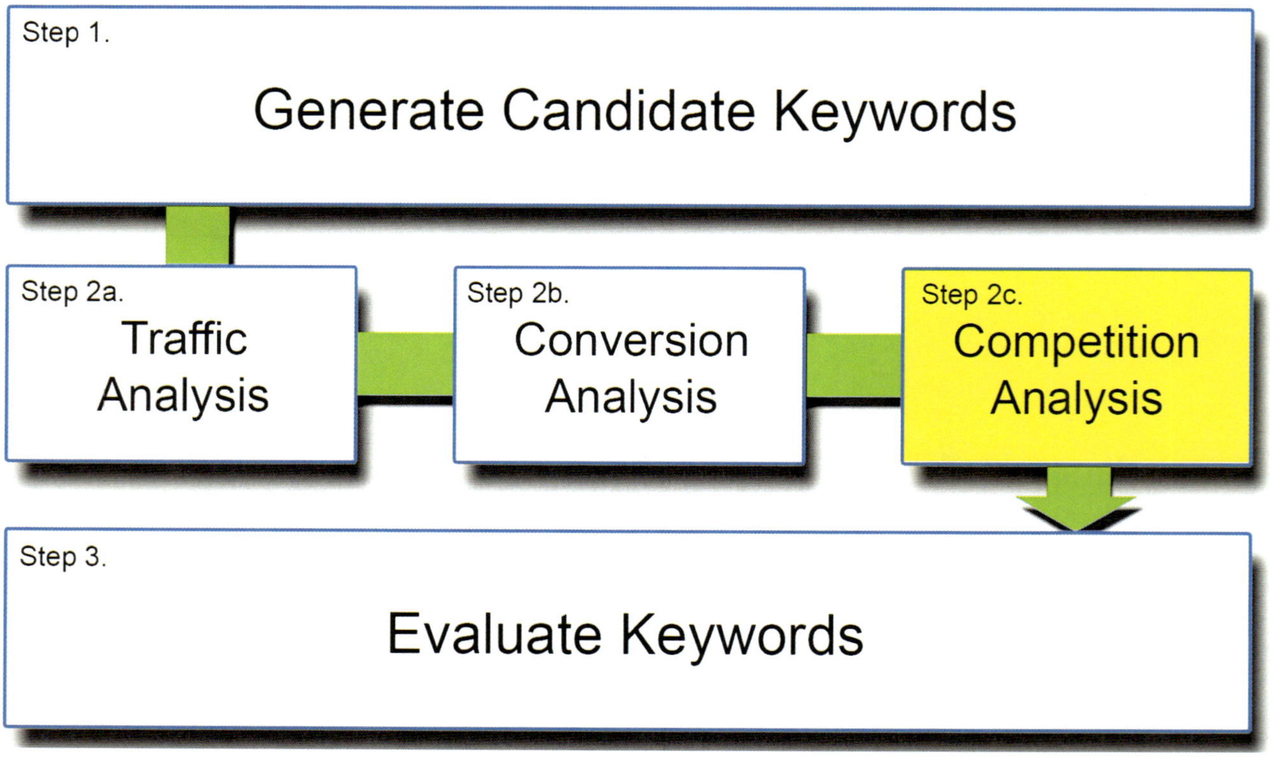

Figure 44 – Competition analysis is step 2c of developing a keyword strategy.

When other websites link to you it is like a vote for your website. Each vote helps your website ascend the search rankings. The most valuable links are those that contain relevant text from trusted sites. For example, to rank well for *silk slippers* an inbound link using the words *silk slippers* from a trusted site like the Wall Street Journal would be highly valuable. A link using the words *click here* from an obscure blog would be less valuable.

Start by benchmarking your site against the incumbent #1 site for the keyword. This comparison is performed across a number of dimensions.

Unique Linking Domains

The number of links going into a website and a webpage are good predictors of search engine success and the level of resource commitment required to overtake the top site in the search engine rankings.

Specifically, you are interested in the number of unique linking domains going into each of the competing pages. The *Unique Linking Domains* metric counts only one link from each domain. For example, if you received 100 links from Mark Cuban's blog, they would be counted as a single link in the Unique Linking Domain metric.

The count of Unique Linking Domains can be found using SEOmoz or Ahrefs. SEOmoz, a subscription based site (http://www.SEOmoz.com/), maintains a link analysis tool called *Open Site Explorer* (http://www.OpenSitexplorer.org/). Ahrefs, also a subscription based site (http://www.ahrefs.com/), maintains a link analysis tool called Site Explorer on it's website. Both these metrics are available for free from the SEObook toolbar.

Figure 45 – Webpage link data on the SEOmoz and SEObook toolbars; (A) SEOmoz unique linking domains, (B) Ahref unique linking domains.

To determine the number of unique linking domains, navigate to the competing page on both your site and your competitor's site and read the number of unique links from the SEO-book toolbar numbers. We prefer using the SEOmoz numbers, but you can also use the Ahrefs numbers, or take an average.

Record your numbers and your competitor's numbers on the *Your Unique Linking Domains* and *Competitor Unique Linking Domains* columns, of the *Competition Analysis* worksheet. From these numbers we calculate the *Link Deficit*, a measure of how many more websites link to your competitors webpage than link to your webpage.

Link Deficit = Competitor's Unique Linking Domains − Your Unique Linking Domains

If the Link Deficit is less than zero, record the score as zero.

For example, if a competitor's *silk slippers* webpage has 92 Unique Linking Domains and your webpage has 28 Unique Linking Domains, the link deficit for the keyword *silk slippers* would be 64.

Link Deficit = Competitor's Unique Linking Domains – Your Unique Linking Domains

= 92 Unique Linking Domains – 28 Unique Linking Domains

= 64 Unique Linking Domains

The link deficit is automatically calculated on the *Competition Analysis* worksheet of your spreadsheet.

The count of unique linking domains is an insightful metric, but it does not capture the quality and type of links. This means that this metric values all links as if they were worth the same, when in reality some links are worth significantly more than others. The metric does not take into account that links from more authoritative pages on more authoritative sites have more SEO power. For example, a link from the homepage of the Wall Street Journal is worth a lot more than a link from an obscure blog post. The metric also does not take into account the link anchor text, and thus values a generic link that uses *click here* the same as a more valuable descriptive link with your exact keyword.

To address these limitations, and take into account the role of link authority and link content, we employ the *Page Authority* metric and *Anchor Text* metric respectively.

Page Authority

Although the number of links is an important data point, you must also understand the quality of inbound links for a robust competitive assessment. To understand the quality of links we use metrics that measure the authority of a page. Authority metrics tell us the degree to which a page's links are coming from trusted sites. The two most commonly used sources for Page Authority information are the *Google PageRank* and *SEOmoz Page Authority*.

Google PageRank - a Google published metric that measures the trust of a page. PageRank is largely driven by the number and quality of links pointing to a page. PageRank is available for free, and the information is integrated into the SEObook toolbar. To view the PageRank of a page, simply navigate to the page and check the SEObook toolbar.

Figure 46 – PageRank score on the SEObook toolbar.

PageRank is updated by Google at irregular intervals. These update intervals average six months, but can be as much as a year apart. Consequently, looking at the PageRank metric often only provides a dated snapshot of a competitor. PageRank is reported on a scale of 1-10, with scores only reported in whole numbers (i.e., 1, 2, 3 ...). Finally, the scale is a log scale, with a base of approximately eight (e.g., a PR 3 has eight times more authority than a PR 2). Thus, two sites with the same PageRank score may be as much as 800% apart. For these reasons, we typically use the SEOmoz Page Authority score.

SEOMoz Page Authority (PA) – SEOmoz calculates a similar metric measuring Page Authority. The metric is more frequently updated than PageRank and is on a more granular

0-100 scale.

The PA score for a webpage can be found by navigating to the webpage in question and reading the score from the SEOmoz toolbar. While some metrics on the SEOmoz toolbar require a paid subscription to access them, PA is available for free.

Record the Page Authority numbers for you and the leading competitor on the *Your Page Authority* and *Competitor Page Authority* columns of the *Competition Analysis* worksheet.

Figure 47 – Page Authority score on the SEOmoz toolbar.

After determining the SEOmoz Page Authority for the relevant webpages on your site and the #1 competitor's site for a given keyword, calculate the *Authority Deficit*. The *Authority Deficit* is a metric used to account for differences in quality of the links:

$$\text{Authority Deficit} = \frac{10^{\left(\frac{\text{Competitor Authority}}{10}\right)} - 10^{\left(\frac{\text{Your Authority}}{10}\right)}}{1000}$$

If the Authority Deficit is less than zero, then record the score as zero.

For example, if your competitor's *silk slippers* webpage has a PA of 62, and your competing webpage has a PA of 58, the authority deficit for the keyword *silk slippers* would be 954 as calculated below.

$$\text{Authority Deficit} = \frac{10^{\left(\frac{\text{Competitor Authority}}{10}\right)} - 10^{\left(\frac{\text{Your Authority}}{10}\right)}}{1000}$$

$$= \frac{10^{\left(\frac{62}{10}\right)} - 10^{\left(\frac{58}{10}\right)}}{1000}$$

$$= 954$$

The authority deficit is automatically calculated on your spreadsheet in the *Authority Deficit* column of the *Competition Analysis* worksheet.

Anchor Text

In addition to the number and quality of the links, the anchor text is important. Anchor text is the clickable text used to create a link (it is usually blue and underlined). While anchor text has become less important in the aftermath of the Google Penguin algorithm update, it is still important for the keyword to appear in the anchor text of a good fraction of the links.

The Importance of Anchor Text: Why Mega Brands Rarely Rank Well

Beating big brands belonging to mega-corporations is often not very difficult. Although you would expect Nike to be a formidable competitor for the keyword *sneakers*, they are not as competitive as you would think, residing outside the top-50.

The primary reason is that very few of the links going to the site use the keywords *sneakers*. Instead, most of these links have *Nike* or some other brand as the anchor text. In fact, of the 50,000 links to Nike, there are only about 10 links with the word *sneaker* as the anchor text. Nike is topped for the keyword *sneaker* by much smaller companies like the obscure online retailer, Dr. Jays. Dr. Jays has only 3,000 links, but has many more links with *sneaker* or some variant as the anchor text.

When assessing the competition, note every link with the exact keyword, or a partial match of the keyword, as a link. For example, if you analyzed the *silk slippers*, you would count not only exact match *silk slippers* anchor text, but also partial matches like *comfy silk slippers*, *comfortable slipper*, *silk slipper*, and *silk shoes* as you determine the anchor text count.

There are two options for evaluating anchor text: Link Diagnosis (free) and SEOmoz Open Site Explorer (paid).

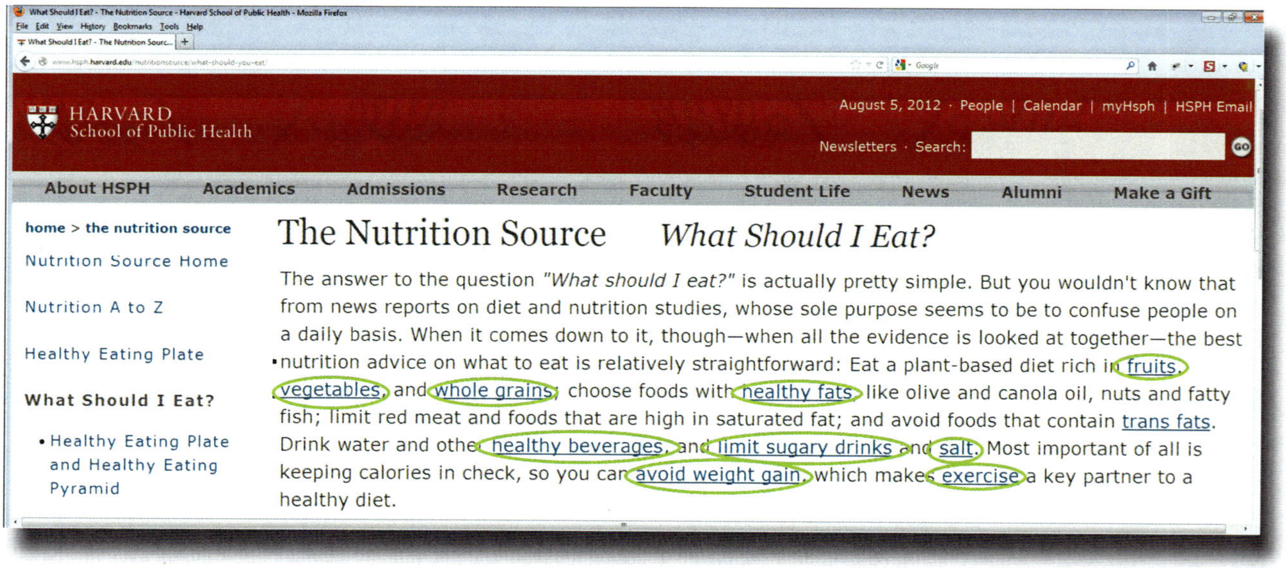

Figure 48 – Examples of anchor text.

Link Diagnosis (free)

Link Diagnosis provides a free link analysis tool. The results displayed by the Link Diagnosis tool are based on SEOmoz Linkscape data, although results are often truncated for sites with a lot of links. For those larger sites you need to extrapolate from the limited results.

Step 1: Link Diagnosis

Go to Link Diagnosis (http://www.linkdiagnosis.com) and download their Firefox toolbar by clicking the *Download the Toolbar* link at the top of the screen. The full data is only available to users who have the toolbar installed, everyone else gets a *lite* version.

> Go to linkdiagnosis.com and download the toolbar.

Step 2: Enter Page

Enter the webpage you want to analyze in the dialog box. In the *Engine* dropdown box select *SEOmoz*, in the *Site Settings* dropdown select *Single Page*, then click *Start*.

> Enter competitor URL, select *SEOmoz*, select *Single Page*, then click *Start*.

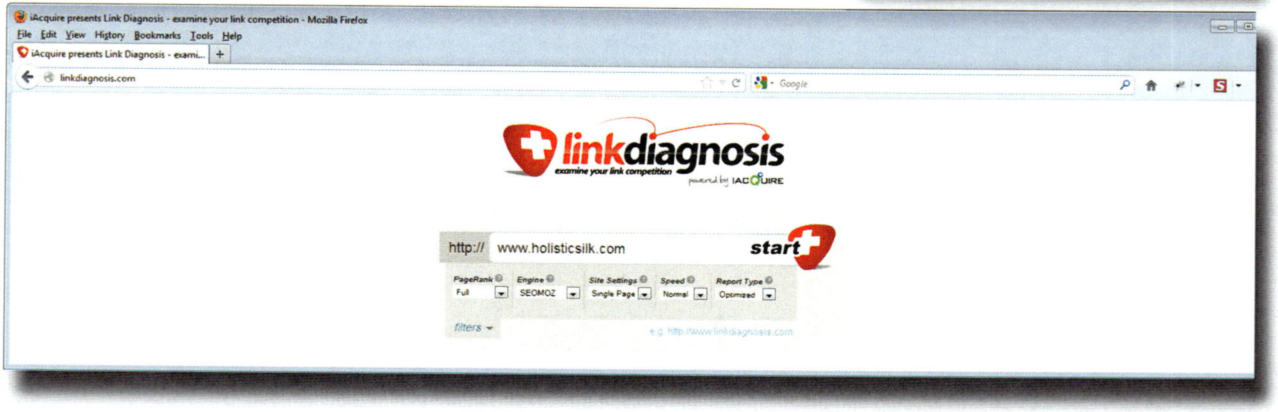

Figure 49 – Enter your target webpage, select *SEOmoz* & *Single Page*, then click *Start*.

Step 3: Download Data

Click on the *Export* button to download the links data.

Click *Export* and save the file.

Step 4: Triage Data

In Excel sort the results by anchor text and comb through the listings, counting any links where there is a partial match between the anchor text and the selected keyword. Record your findings for the number of anchor text links for your website and your leading competitors' websites on the *Your Anchor Links* and *Competitor Anchor Links* columns on the *Competition Analysis* worksheet.

Tally matching links.

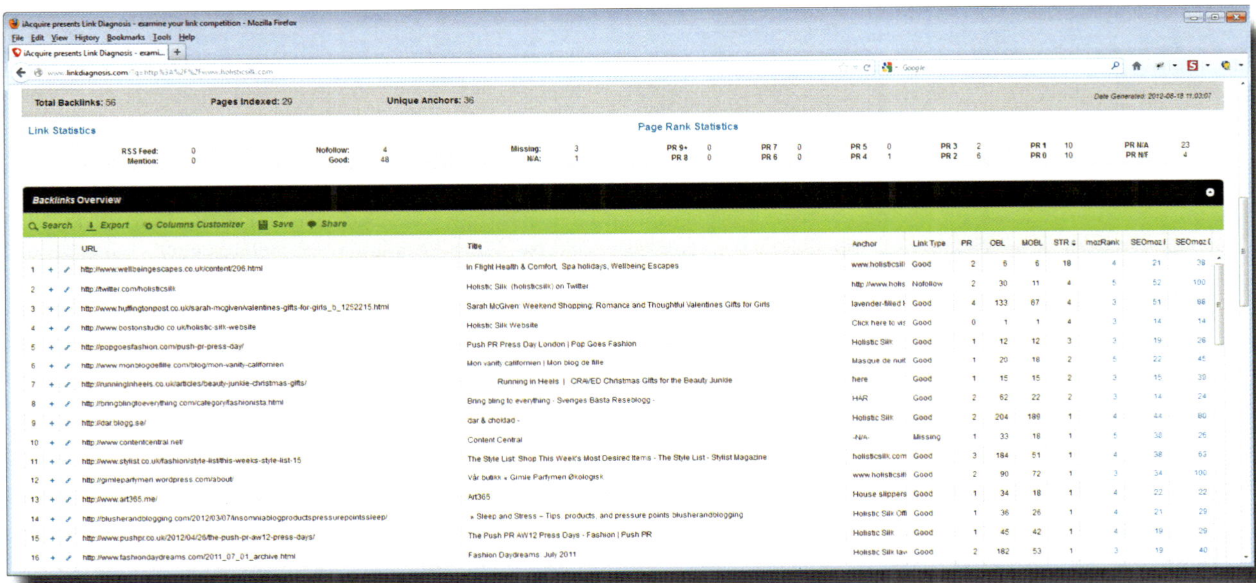

Figure 50 – Link Diagnosis results.

Open Site Explorer (paid)

SEOmoz includes a tool called Open Site Explorer (OSE). The full tool is only available with their $100 per month subscription. The unpaid version is not useful for this analysis.

Step 1: Login

Navigate to Open Site Explorer (http://OpenSiteExplorer.org/) and login using the *Login* link on the top right of the screen.

Go to opensiteexplorer.org and login.

Step 2: Enter Page

Enter the address of the webpage you are analyzing in the white search bar at the top of the page, then click the *Search* button.

Enter webpage URL and click *Search*.

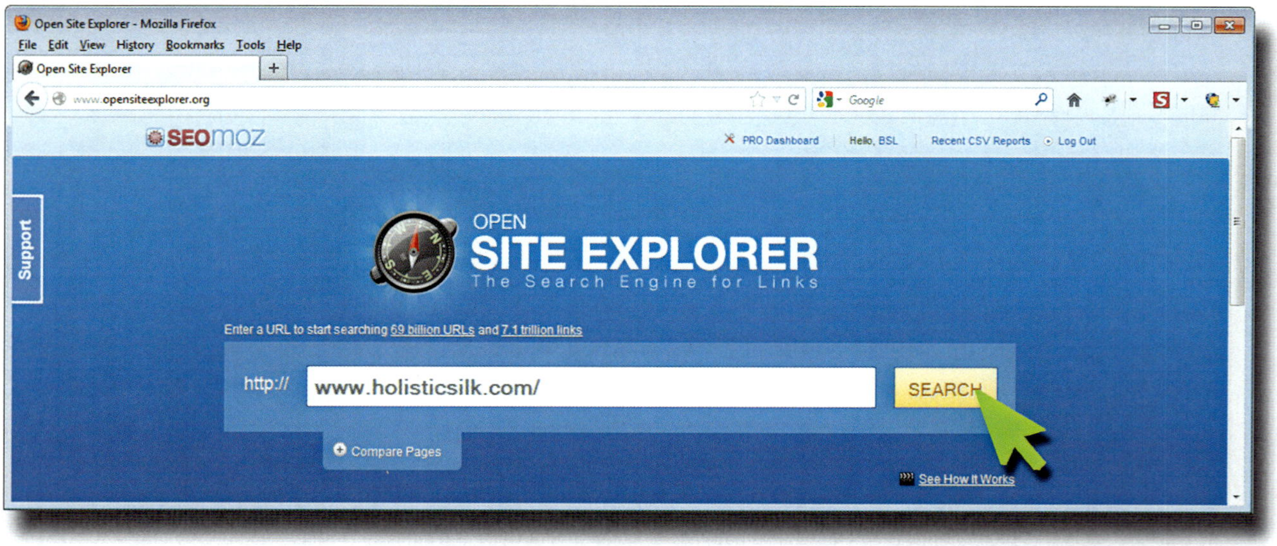

Figure 51 – Enter the webpage for analysis in the Open Site Explorer search bar.

Step 3: Collect Data

Click the *Anchor Text* tab and check to make sure that the settings under the tabs are *Show anchor text phrases for links to this page*.

Click *Anchor Text* tab, and click *Download CSV* icon.

Download the data to Microsoft Excel by clicking the *Download CSV* button and saving the file that is produced.

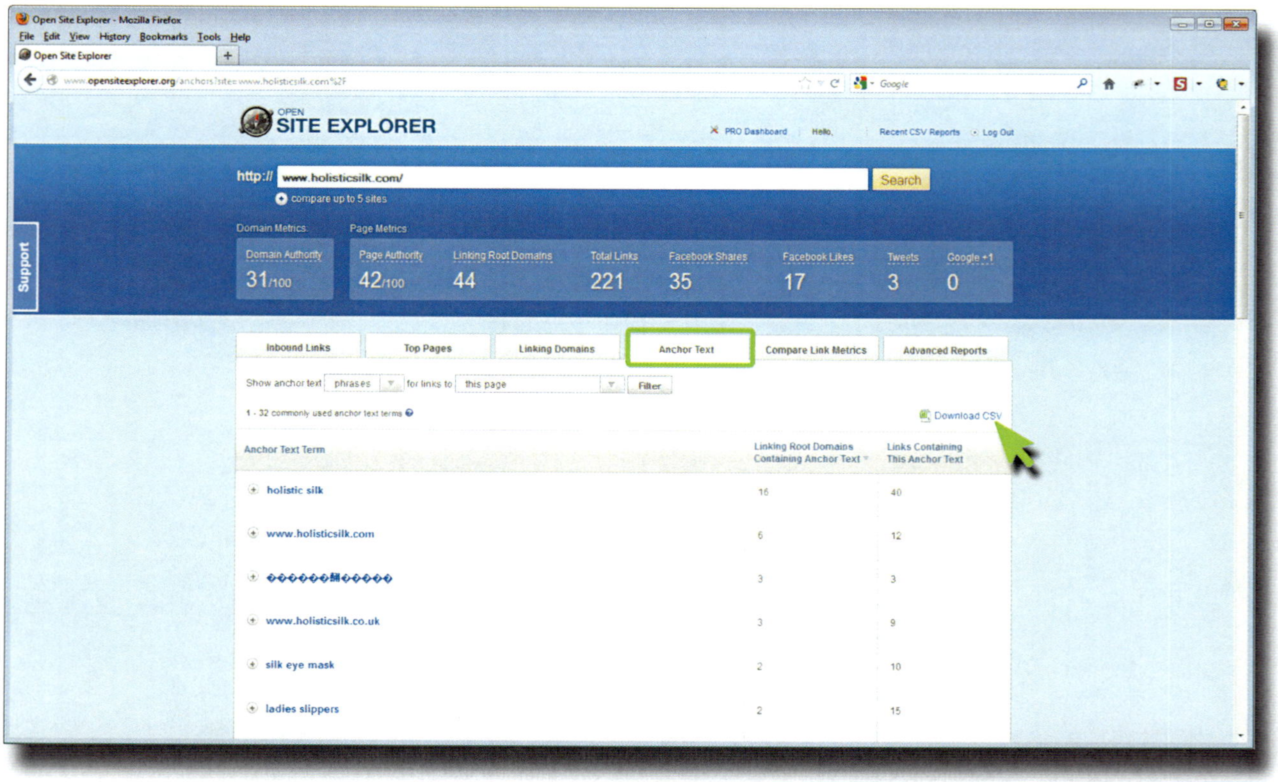

Figure 52 – Download the anchor text results from Open Site Explorer.

Beware of the Exact Match URL

A competitor with an exact match URL will have a huge competitive advantage when it comes to winning that keyword. This is because Google gives a large boost to websites whose URLs match the search term. For example, if you are competing for the keyword *silk slippers* and your competitor has the website www.silkslippers.com, then that website needs an order of magnitude fewer links to rank well for that keyword. Exact match URLs also benefit because links to the site will usually use the site name which hits the targeted anchor text.

Exact match competitors can be beaten if the competitor is not doing any serious link building. But, if the competitor is serious about SEO, they can win that keyword with a fraction of the work that it would take you to win and are practically unbeatable. Consequently, it is rarely wise to compete against a SEO-savvy competitor with an exact match URL for the #1 position for that exact match keyword.

Step 4: Triage Data

Tally matching links using linking *root domains* column

Sort through the anchor text to find anchor text that fully or partially matches the target keyword. Use the numbers in the first column *Linking Root Domains Containing Anchor Text* for link totals, as this metric counts multiple links from a single domain only once.

Record the number of anchor text links for your website and your competitors' websites on the *Your Anchor Links* and *Competitor Anchor Links* columns on the *Competition Analysis* worksheet.

From this data calculate the anchor text deficit. Compare the number of match and partial match anchor text links in your site to that of the #1 ranked competitor for the keyword.

Anchor Deficit = Competitor Anchor Links - Your Anchor Links

If the Anchor Deficit is less than zero, record the score as zero.

For example, if your competitor's *silk slippers* webpage has 71 matching or partially matching anchor text links and your competing webpage has 27 matching or partially matching anchor text links, the Anchor Text Deficit for the keyword *silk slippers* would be 44.

Anchor Text Deficit = Competitor Anchors Links - Your Anchor Links

= 71 - 27

= 44

The *Anchor Text Deficit* is automatically calculated on your spreadsheet in the *Anchor Deficit* column.

Competitive Factor

To outrank a competitor you need more links or better links than the competitor. Unfortunately, by the time you build your links (for a large link building campaign you will want to spread the link building over 1-2 years for efficacy and logistical reasons), the competitor will also have acquired more links. As you ascend the rankings, an SEO-savvy competitor will notice and respond by increasing their rate of link building.

The competition is not a static target and will often react to your SEO efforts by ramping up their own efforts to defend their position. When a competitor notices you are overtaking or threatening to overtake their ranking, they will often increase their link building velocity. In most cases, a determined competitor can match any SEO efforts you put in, and then some.

To account for the different competitive reactions in the marketplace, incorporate a *Competitive Factor* into your SEO cost equations. The Competitive Factor accounts for the different levels of competition across different keywords.

Examine competitor link profiles to get an idea of how SEO-savvy they may be. On their primary pages, examine the text and meta-data (see Chapter 2) to assess if the pages are rich in relevant keywords. Also, take a deep look at their links (see Chapter 5), and judge if the links appear to have been unsolicited, or whether they look less natural and appear to be the result of proactive link building. Aggressive competitors will boast keyword rich pages and appear to be active link builders.

Competitor SEO	Factor
No SEO (no keywords on pages, no active link building)	1.0
Casual SEO (keywords on pages, minimal link building)	2.0
Serious SEO (keyword rich text, heavy link building)	3.0

Table 3 – Competitive Factors by competitor type.

For example, a 1.2 competitive factor is appropriate for a sleepy competitor that is not actively link building and is unlikely to respond to your link building efforts with link building of their own. For a competitor that does a bit of SEO via automated link building, 1.5 is more reasonable. For a more SEO aggressive competitor that we expect to retaliate to aggressive link building with their own aggressive link building, estimate a factor of 3 or higher.

Enter these competitive factors for your keyword in the *Competition Analysis* worksheet in the *Competitive Factor* column of the spreadsheet.

Calculating SEO Cost

Combine the link, anchor text, authority, and competition data for each keyword to generate an estimate of the cost of an SEO campaign. This estimate represents the cost to take the #1 position from a competitor, and is calculated using the following equation:

$$\text{Cost} = (50 \times \text{Link Deficit} + 30 \times \text{Authority Deficit} + 500 \times \text{Anchor Deficit}) \times \text{Competitive Factor}$$

For example, if for the keyword *silk slippers*, your Link Deficit was 64, your Authority Deficit was 954, your Anchor Text Deficit was 44, and the Competitive Factor was 1.9, then the estimated cost of taking the #1 position for the keyword is $102,000.

$$\text{Cost} = (50 \times \text{Link Deficit} + 30 \times \text{Authority Deficit} + 500 \times \text{Anchor Deficit}) \times \text{Competitive Factor}$$

$$= (50 \times 64 + 30 \times 954 + 500 \times 44) \times 1.9$$

$$= \$102{,}000$$

How Much Does a Link Cost?

Although Google prohibits the direct purchase of links, there are a variety of link building techniques that satisfy Google's directives. Most of these techniques have significant labor costs associated with them. Link building is largely a social activity and, as such, a worker who is a native speaker and has a high social IQ is typically more successful than an outsourced non-native speaker.

The cost of building a medium quality link is approximately $100 when you use one of the more reputable link building techniques. The bulk

continued

> of the cost is labor driven. For this amount, you could get a guest post on a real PageRank 3 blog that has real readers and an average of one to two comments on each post.
>
> There are also a variety of cheaper automated techniques that build links. These links will fool the search engines for a while, but inevitably search engines catch on. Therefore these tactics are only valuable for the short term. And if used, these tactics should be blended with higher quality techniques. These techniques cost approximately $10 per link, including labor costs.

Costs are generally higher where link building is particularly difficult. Link building is difficult when the keyword you are promoting is a boring or taboo topic, because it is harder to find linking partners. Costs are generally lower where link building is centered on an interesting topic, particularly a topic that is going to be interesting to the blogosphere. For example, the keyword *silk slippers* is going to be relatively easy to build links because it is related to women's clothing—a topic that will be a good fit with female fashion and lifestyle bloggers. So, we would expect the cost to be a little lower than the predicted $102,000.

Keyword Synergy Savings

There are cost savings when you optimize the same page for multiple keywords because you have already overcome the link and anchor text deficits for the first keyword. Therefore, these parts of the optimization are less daunting for the second keyword.

To perform the analysis for multiple keywords, first perform the basic cost analysis for the keyword with the largest link deficit and the largest authority deficit. But, for the second and subsequent keywords, use the following two formulas.

Overlapping Keywords

When optimizing multiple keywords that are similar, the link building is often synergistic. For example, links for *seat covers* will also help you win *car seat covers* and *seat protectors*. If there is an overlap of keywords being optimized for the same page on your website, the cost of the second and subsequent keywords should be discounted to account for the overlap. Calculate the cost of the second and subsequent keywords using the following formula:

$$\text{Cost} = (10 \times \text{Link Deficit} + 6 \times \text{Authority Deficit} + 250 \times \text{Anchor Deficit}) \times \text{Competition Factor}$$

For example, if you performed the SEO cost analysis for *silk slippers*, and wanted to determine the additional cost to SEO *pink silk slippers* a keyword where you had a link deficit of 7, an authority deficit of 300 and an anchor text deficit of 5, then the cost for this second keyword would be $6,000:

Cost = (10 × Link Deficit + 6 × Authority Deficit + 250 × Anchor Deficit) × Competition Factor

Cost = (10 × 7 + 6 × 300 + 250 × 5) × 1.9

= $5,928

Note that the cost of doing *silk slippers* by itself would be $22,500. By optimizing for *silk slippers* along with the singular *silk slipper* you save almost 75%.

Non-Overlapping Keywords

Optimizing for different keywords that do not overlap results in synergy; but not as much as the synergy of overlapping keywords. For non-overlapping keywords, use the formula:

Cost = (10 × Link Deficit + 6 × Authority Deficit + 500 × Anchor Deficit) × Competition Factor

Assume you had already performed the SEO cost analysis for *silk slippers* and wanted to determine the additional costs for *soft shoes*. For *soft shoes* there is a link deficit of 64, an authority deficit of 650 and an anchor text deficit of 30. The cost for this second keyword would be $37,700 and calculated as follows:

Cost = (10 × Link Deficit + 6 × Authority Deficit + 500 × Anchor Deficit) × Competition Factor

= (10 × 30 + 6 × 650 + 500 × 30) × 1.9

= $36,480

Note that the cost of doing *soft shoes* by itself is $68,400. Adding *silk slippers* results in approximately 50% savings based on the overlap in work to cure the link deficit and the authority deficit.

If there are lower costs due to synergy, you will need to manually enter them in the *SEO Cost* column of the spreadsheet.

Reducing SEO Costs

The cost calculations assume the use of conventional SEO link building tactics. But, in some situations there are lower cost alternatives.

Acquisitions and Partnerships

As an alternative to battling for search rank through SEO, consider acquiring or partnering with sites that have superior rankings. Acquiring top ranking sites is often more cost effective and almost always faster than outperforming them in SEO. Acquisition or partnership should be considered, particularly if the top sites are not efficiently converting their traffic into profit, as is often the case with informational sites that are monetizing using advertising.

These sites will often be open to selling their site or traffic at a discount to the SEO cost of the traffic.

Black Hat SEO

The cost of SEO can be lowered about 50% by engaging in more risky link building techniques. The search engines establish guidelines for how to build links and prohibit certain techniques such as paying for links and using private blog networks. However, many of these prohibited techniques are effective and the risk of detection is low. Thus, using these *black hat* techniques allows you to increase search rank at a lower cost than using conventional link building techniques.

The formula used in this book assumes that you will largely be practicing the more conservative *white hat* SEO that complies with search engine guidelines. But, an SEO practitioner willing to take on more risk could layer in black hat techniques and halve costs. The tradeoff is that there is a chance that these prohibited techniques will be discovered and penalized by the search engines. Black hat SEO also tends to last for a shorter time because search engines continuously update their algorithm to mitigate the impact of these tactics.

In this chapter and the previous two chapters we have estimated the traffic, conversion, and cost associated with SEO for specific keywords. In the next chapter we pull together these analyses to estimate the payback period for SEO for each keyword and enable comparisons between keywords.

6 Evaluate Keywords

Summary: Calculate a Payback Period for each keyword under consideration by combining the analysis from the previous sections. Use the payback metrics to:

- **Compare Keywords** – Compare the returns from SEO for individual keywords and guide SEO resource allocation between keywords.

- **Compare Opportunities** – Compare the returns from SEO to other potential business initiatives and guide resource allocation between these opportunities.

"Price is what you pay; value is what you get. Whether we're talking about socks or stocks, I like buying quality merchandise when it is marked down."

Warren Buffet, *Investor* (1929 -).

By combining the analyses from the previous three chapters, compute a Payback Period for each keyword. This enables you to evaluate SEO keyword opportunities, prioritize high return keywords, and discard low return keywords. It also enables you to evaluate how attractive the SEO opportunities are in your industry and how SEO compares to other investment opportunities in your portfolio of initiatives.

Payback Period is calculated by dividing the forecasted profit by the SEO cost. Payback periods of less than two years are highly attractive. Payback Periods of two to four years are viable, depending on the availability of business capital and the Payback Period of competing business activities. SEO opportunities with Payback Periods exceeding four years should be avoided.

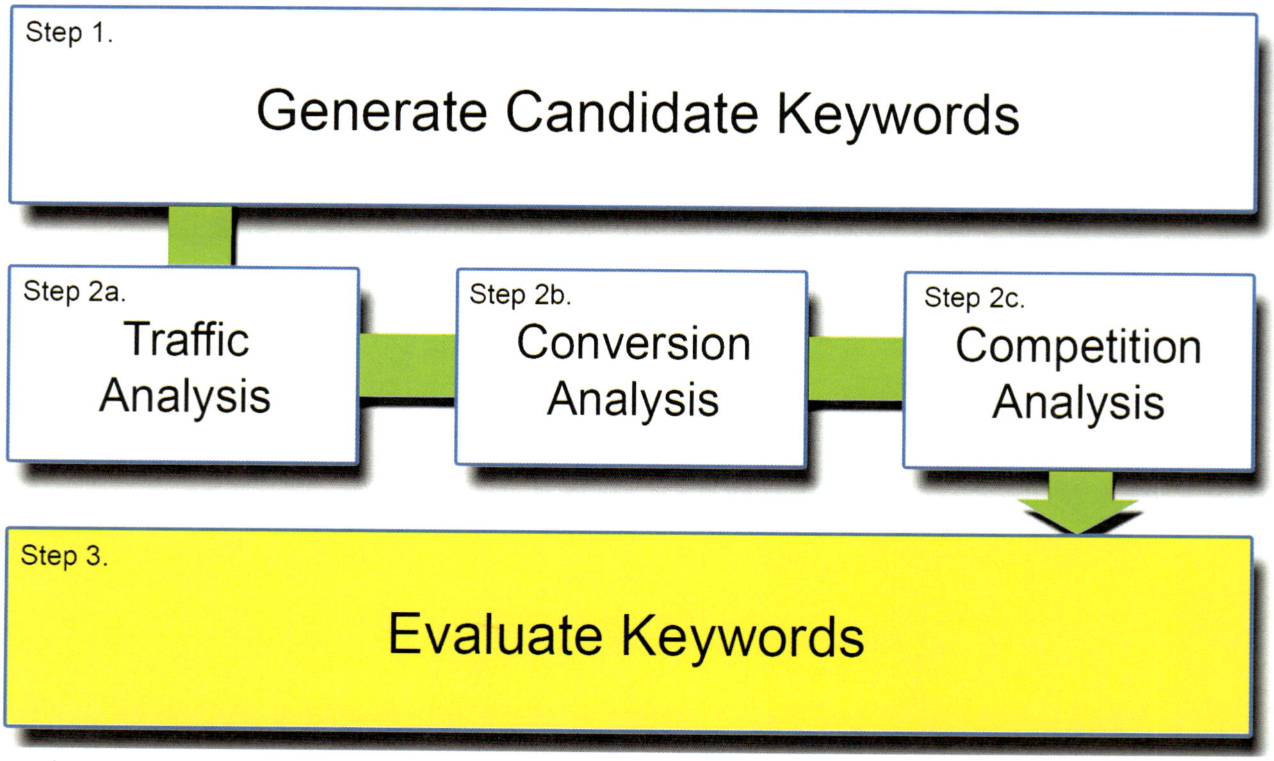

Figure 53 – Evaluating keywords is the final step in developing a keyword strategy.

Use the Payback Period in conjunction with business judgment to create a shortlist of keywords for search engine optimization. While the Payback Period metric is not dispositive, it is a useful aid for decision making.

Calculating the Payback Period

Payback Period measures the time required to be repaid your original investment. Payback Period is calculated by dividing the projected cost of the SEO work required to reach the #1 search position (or other desired rank) by the projected increase in annual profit.

$$\text{Payback Period} = \frac{\text{SEO Cost}}{\text{Incremental Annual Profit}} = \frac{\text{SEO Cost}}{\text{Total Cost} \times \text{Conversion}}$$

We forecasted that winning *silk slippers* would result in an additional 21,600 searches per month, and that each search resulted in an additional $0.14 in profit over the lifetime of the customer. This results in a Payback Period of 3.9 making this a reasonable, but unspectacular project.

$$\begin{aligned}\text{Payback Period} &= \frac{\text{SEO Cost}}{\text{Total Cost} \times \text{Conversion}} \\ &= \frac{\$106{,}000}{25{,}000 \text{ searches/year} \times \$1.10\text{/search}} \\ &\approx 3.9 \text{ years}\end{aligned}$$

Exact Numbers Do Not Imply Precision!

This book, and in particular this chapter, provides a methodology for analyzing keyword opportunities and quantifying the Payback Period for these opportunities. While you will get seemingly precise estimates using these methods, these estimates add a deceptive veneer of accuracy to a fundamentally imprecise art.

Like all business forecasting, underneath the precise formulas lies some voodoo. When evaluating keywords, we implicitly rely on soft knowledge and experience. SEO algorithms are in flux from year-to-year, competitor reactions to a threat are unpredictable, customer demand can be fickle, and all that uncertainty is hidden from view by the formulas.

continued

> We aim to err on the side of conservatism. But, we are continually humbled by our inability to forecast the future with any great level of precision when optimizing our sites and those of our clients. Some SEO campaigns unexpectedly turn out to be a stroll in the park, and others reveal themselves to be a death march.
>
> We estimate the 80% confidence interval for the payback calculation, to be -50% / +100%. For example, if the forecasted Payback Period is two years, our 80% confidence interval should be between one (2 × [1 - 50%]) and four (2 × [1 + 100%]) years.

Interpreting the Payback Period

When interpreting the Payback Period and deciding whether to greenlight an SEO project, pay special attention to the return likely to be generated from the investment.

SEO should be treated as a high risk investment because of the search engine uncertainty and the competitive uncertainty. The changing nature of the Google search algorithm rules creates risk. Google and the other search engines can, and do, change the way they rank sites. When Google makes changes to their algorithm to improve the quality of search results and combat webspam, there are innocent bystander casualties. The competitive nature of SEO also creates risk. When you win #1 for a keyword, you take traffic away from a competitor and that competitor may react by ramping up their SEO efforts. This can escalate into an arms race where everyone is spending ever-increasing amounts on SEO to fight over a fixed pool of customers.

However, along with the greater risk comes greater opportunity. Given the risk and lack of transparency, there are many market inefficiencies where traffic can be acquired at a small fraction of the cost of revenue. These are opportunities that would quickly disappear in more efficient markets. Most companies are still not doing any SEO, and even fewer are doing SEO well. Due to the aforementioned rule uncertainty many companies are unwilling to invest in SEO because it is too murky. In this environment there are many bargains lying around. Opportunities and investment in SEO can yield eye-popping returns. Return on investment figures of 500% are not unusual in SEO — returns that are not possible in the more efficient and lower risk Pay-Per-Click markets where 10% is often considered a good return.

This means that you should expect high returns on SEO expenditures and should be unwilling to spend on marginally attractive SEO campaigns.

We suggest you only undertake SEO opportunities where the Payback Period is less than four years. Where the Payback Period is less than two years, the project fits in the no-brainer category. Where the Payback Period is between two and four years, the project should be evaluated in light of other business opportunities and only approved if either capital is plentiful or other opportunities are less appealing. And, if the Payback Period is greater than four years, the project should not be undertaken unless there is strategic rationale for the project that provides additional benefit not captured by the analyses.

Payback Period	Guidance
0 - 2 years	Excellent opportunity for SEO. Proceed with project immediately!
2 - 4 years	Good opportunity for SEO. Evaluate SEO opportunity in the context of other growth opportunities in your business.
4 + years	Insufficient return. Proceed only if other strategic factors create a compelling rationale for SEO.

Table 4 – Evaluating the Payback Period.

SEO Opportunities are Relative

Where SEO does not make financial sense for you, the question often arises as to why it does makes sense for competitors. There are five reasons why a competitor might be pursuing SEO when the opportunity does not look as attractive to a new entrant.

Lower Costs - SEO may cost your competitors less than it would cost you, particularly if you are a new entrant. A longtime online business enjoys the luxury of having accumulated a large number of links over the lifetime of their website. Some competitors also find it easier to attract links, this being particularly true of competitors that have a strong offline brand.

Higher Rewards - SEO might have a greater payback for your competitor than it does for you. A competitor might be more efficient at converting traffic into customers, they might be able to extract more revenue out of customers over the lifetime of the relationship, and they may have higher margins due to differences in their cost structure. If you sell razors, and a competitor sells razors plus shaving cream, they can afford to pay more to acquire a customer in the knowledge that they will be able to upsell some fraction of their customers to the shaving cream.

Higher Risk Tolerance - a competitor might simply be acting with a more aggressive risk profile. They may be willing to take bigger risks or they may be betting on other factors to bail them out. When we told you to be dissatisfied with a Payback Period over four years, they may be satisfied with a longer Payback Period because they have excess capital or lower opportunity costs.

Escalating Commitment – competitors can get trapped in cycles of escalating commitment. The number two site for a keyword can double traffic by investing a little more in SEO and edging past the #1 site (going from 15% of the organic clicks to 42%). This can, in turn, trigger the deposed #1 site to retaliate by investing a little more in SEO. In this way, the leading sites can find themselves trapped in a never-ending cycle of increased SEO investment.

Irrationality – finally, a competitor might simply be acting irrationally. Not everyone you compete against created a detailed keyword strategy, and many business people navigate by instinct. This is a faster approach and has many merits, but it does lead to some bad decisions where you embark on projects which a wiser person would pass up.

SEO in Context

When interpreting the results of these analyses, it is important to consider SEO in the context of the broader objective of marketing. SEO is one of many marketing techniques, and where SEO opportunities look bleak, other marketing opportunities may be promising.

In the Internet marketing arena there are many other opportunities including Pay-Per-Click advertising, social media, banner ads, email/list marketing, and peer-to-peer marketing. In addition to the online opportunities, there is a world of offline marketing opportunities.

7 Conclusion

We hope this book provides a conceptual framework for generating a keyword strategy. Our approach is essentially a cost-benefit analysis comparing the payoff from improving search rank to the cost of the activities required to create this improvement.

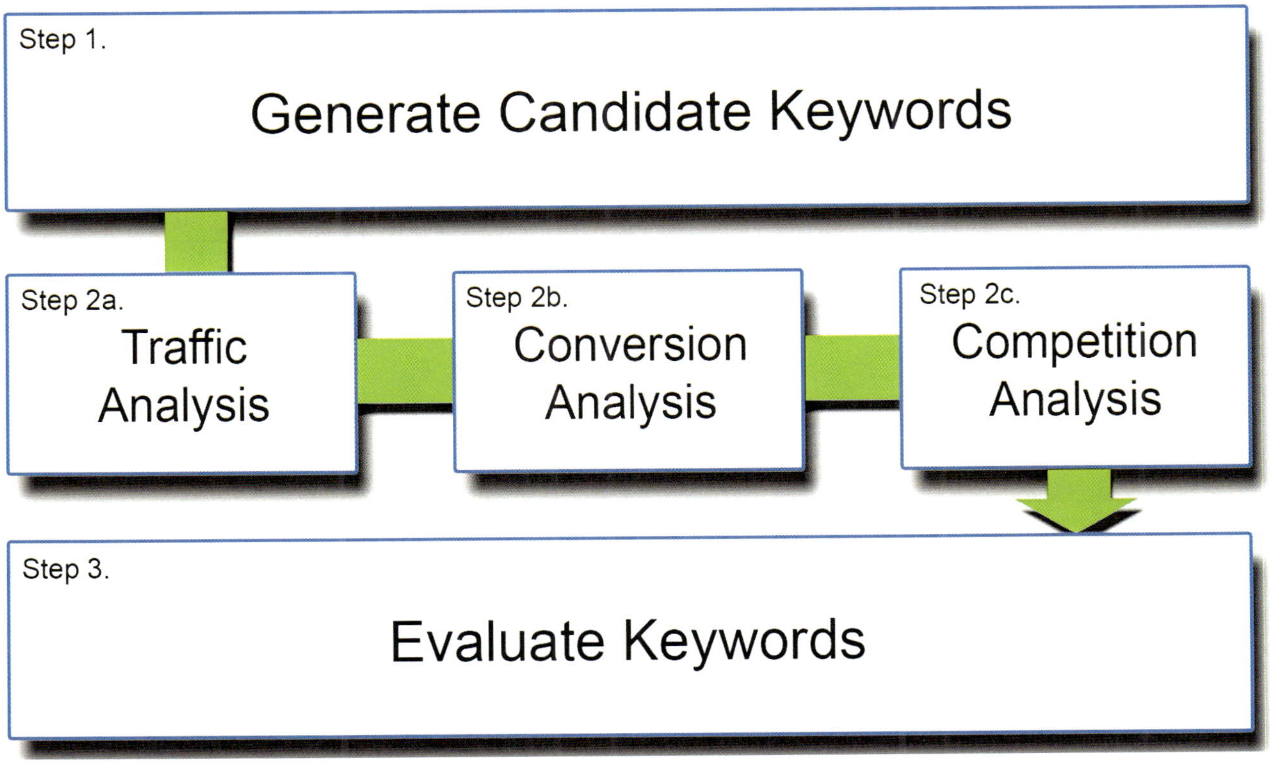

Figure 54 – The keyword strategy process.

The practical framework for forecasting the payback period for specific keywords starts with the generation of a broad set of relevant candidate keywords. For each keyword, a traffic and conversion analysis is performed to forecast the incremental profit that will result from improved search rank. Then, a competitive analysis is done to estimate the costs of overtaking the competition. Finally, these analyses are combined to evaluate each keyword's payback period.

You are now equipped to perform a rigorous analysis of keywords and set the keyword strategy for your business. The final ingredient is experience.

Keyword strategy is as much art as it is science. While you strive to be data driven, you must constantly rely on estimates. The ever-changing rules also complicate matters. The formulas provided in this book are based on the experience of the authors and our clients. Recognize that your industry and/or niche will be different.

Remember to consistently document your keyword data and analysis as part of the process. We encourage you to reflect on this analysis every six months, comparing predictions to actual results and calibrating accordingly. Periodic review will enhance your expertise and judgment related to the intricacies of your industry and SEO in general.

Finally, we invite you to continue the SEO discussion. This book started as part of our internal training program. As such, this book, and indeed any book on this topic, must be considered merely part of a lifelong apprenticeship and an element of a larger conversation about keyword strategy and SEO.

Video tutorials covering all the topics in this book can be found at http://www.seomap.com/seo/keyword-strategy/. The tutorials provide a refresher on the material and walk through real-life examples. The website also includes downloadable keyword strategy worksheets and slides (http://www.seomap.com/seo/keyword-strategy/spreadsheet/). To keep up to date on everything SEO subscribe to our blog (http://www.seomap.com/blog).

Let's make this a two-way conversation, so email your questions, comments, and tips to book@seomap.com.

Appendix One: SEO Toolbars Quickstart

SEOmoz Toolbar

(A) **SEOmoz** - SEOmoz.com content.

(B) **Page Authority** – an SEOmoz generated score from 0 (worst) to 100 (best) ranking the authority of the webpage. The score is on a logarithmic scale.

(C) **Page Links** – the number of links to the webpage.

(D) **Page Root Domain Links** – the number of unique domains linking to the webpage.

(E) **Domain Authority** – an SEOmoz score from 0 (worst) to 100 (best) ranking the authority of the domain (website). The score is on a logarithmic scale.

(F) **Domain Links** – the number of links going to a domain (website).

(G) **Root Domain Links** – the number of unique domains linking to a domain (website).

(H) **Tools** – links to various SEOmoz tools.

(I) **Analysis** – displays floating window with consolidated analysis of the page and inbound links.

(J) **Highlight** – highlight keywords and different types of links.

(K) **Country** – the country where the website IP address originates.

(L) **Settings** – configure settings for the SEOmoz toolbar.

(M) **Help**

Get the SEOmoz toolbar at: http://www.seomoz.org/seo-toolbar.

SEObook Toolbar

(A) **SEObook** – options and settings.

(B) **Information Symbol** – assorted metrics for the website.

(C) **Google PageRank** – a score from 0 (lowest) to 10 (highest) indicating the authority of the webpage. Scores are on a log scale, so a page with a score of 4 is approximately 8 times more authoritative than a page with a score of 5.

(D) **Blekko Page Links** – the number of unique domains linking to the current webpage according to the Blekko search service.

(E) **Open Site Explorer Page Links** – the number of unique domains linking to the webpage according to the Open Site Explorer (SEOmoz) service.

(F) **Ahref Page Links** - the number of unique domains linking to the webpage according to the Ahrefs service.

(G) **Majestic SEO Site Links** – the number of pages linking to the website according to the Majestic SEO service.

(H) **Blekko Site Links** – the number of unique domains linking to a website according to the Blekko search service.

(I) **Ahref Site Links** - the number of unique domains linking to the website according to the Ahrefs service

(J) **Open Site Explorer Site Links** – the number of unique domains linking to the domain (website) according to the Open Site Explorer (SEOmoz) service.

(K) **Majestic SEO Unique Site Links** - the number of unique domains linking to the domain (website) according to the Majestic SEO service.

(L) **Blekko Rank** - a Blekko metric for the authority of the domain (website). The scale is linear, and there is no maximum.

(M) **Directory Information** – the inclusion of the website in four major web directories (DMOZ, Yahoo Directory, Best of the Web, & Business.com).

(N) **Domain Age** – the age of the domain (website) according to archive.org.

(O) **Unique Visitors** – the number of monthly unique visitors to the website according to Compete.com.

(P) **Traffic Value** – the monthly value of organic traffic (in US dollars) to the website according to the SEMrush.com service.

(Q) **Competitive Analysis Tools** – links to various metrics and benchmarking sites.

(R) **Search Engine Rank Checker** – a tool for checking the Organic Search Rank of a website.

(S) **SEO XRay** – a tool for performing a keyword density analysis of the web-page.

(T) **View Source** – displays the source code for the website in a new tab.

(U) **Box** – used for the following three tools.

(V) **Keyword Suggest** – a tool for generating keywords based on an initial suggestion.

(W) **Highlight** – highlights all mentions of the keyword on the webpage.

(X) **SEObook** – searches SEObook for content.

(Y) **SEO RSS Feeds** – links to recent articles published by leading SEO blogs.

(Z) **NoFollow** – highlights all nofollow links on the webpage.

(1) **Compare** - compares metrics across two or more websites.

Get the SEObook toolbar at: tools.seobook.com/seo-toolbar/.

SEOmap

SEOmap brings transparency to SEO. Our goal is to improve the quality of search results by helping best-of-breed companies get to the top through access to better information.

Gajan Retnasaba is a Partner at SEOmap, counseling clients on SEO strategy and implementation. Gajan owns and operates several ecommerce companies that have won and retain search dominance in their space. Previously, Gajan was a consultant at McKinsey & Company, advising Fortune 500 clients on strategy. Gajan holds a JD from the Harvard Law School, and an engineering degree from the University of New South Wales (Australia). He has been admitted to the New York bar.

Thomas Parker is a Partner at SEOmap, counseling clients on SEO strategy and implementation. Thomas has extensive experience in starting and growing ecommerce companies. Thomas has experience in business development and was a consultant at McKinsey & Company where he worked with multiple Fortune 500 companies. Thomas received his MBA from the Harvard Business School and a BBA in Finance from the University of North Texas. He is also a Certified Public Accountant.

Meyling Lau is a Partner at SEOmap, leading implementation of enterprise scale link-building programs for clients. Formerly, Mey led a variety of grassroots marketing projects for Hotels.com. Most notably Mey led the Hotels.com Expert Evaluation and Rating Program, the largest and most successful verified hotel reviews database with over one million reviews collected in under a year. Mey is a graduate of the Southern Methodist University.

Made in United States
North Haven, CT
04 November 2026

21723866R00060